The
Yorktown
Victory Monument

The YORKTOWN Victory Monument

Maria G. Hepner

THE History PRESS

Published by The History Press
Charleston, SC
www.historypress.com

Front cover: Yorktown Monument, Yorktown, Virginia, circa 1902. *Library of Congress.*

First published 2021

Manufactured in the United States

ISBN 9781467150514

Library of Congress Control Number: 2021941053

A Dedication and a Debt of Gratitude to My Friend
Derold W. Macclammy
Who told me I should write a book, every day for over twelve years.

Also my great appreciation and thanks to Linda Williams and Robbie Smith for their years of encouragement and faith in me, along with all the staff and volunteers I have met over the years at Colonial National Historical Park.

Contents

Prologue	9
Part I. Centennial "Awe and Disappointment"	13
Part II. Sesquicentennial "Speculation and Preservation"	63
Part III. Septaquintaquinquecentennial "Art and Artifacts"	95
Part IV. Bicentennial "Commemorations and Aspirations"	135
Notes	161
Bibliography	167
Index	173
About the Author	176

Prologue

The war for American independence officially started at Lexington in 1775 with "the shot heard 'round the world," but the Declaration of Independence; the assistance of French, Spanish and Dutch allies; and six years of war had brought George Washington and the Continental Army no closer to victory over the British. Fighting the war on two fronts, Washington battled the British throughout the New England states, and in the South, his trusted generals chased the enemy around the Carolinas. By the summer of 1781, the Continental Army was wearing thin, out of supplies, out of money and out of time. Washington despondently wrote, "Now or never our deliverance must come." Then came news of French naval support sailing toward the Chesapeake Bay and intelligence sent by the Marquis de Lafayette from Virginia.

In August 1781, British naval ships dropped anchor in the harbor of the tobacco trading port of Yorktown. Lieutenant General Charles, Lord Cornwallis, was converging a combined force of nearly eight thousand. Regiments he had marched from the Carolinas joined with another complement formally under the command of Benedict Arnold in Virginia, augmented by Hessian troops, and a colony of army camp followers all trailed by a mass of liberated and runaway slaves. They arrived by ship and overland with wagon trains from their former position at Portsmouth to form a supply base and garrison at the port of Yorktown and across the narrows of the river at Gloucester Point. Here Cornwallis awaited further instructions from his superior, Major General Sir Henry Clinton, and the

Illman Brothers, "The Surrender of Cornwallis at Yorktown, A.D. 1781," 1870.
Library of Congress.

reinforcements of the navy expected to arrive from New York. Having advance warning, most residents of the village seaport evacuated, taking all they could to save from depredations by the coming occupation of the British army.

Upon arrival, the army—using those formerly enslaved followers—set about building fortifications around Yorktown. Houses and other buildings around the outskirts of the town were torn down and their rubble used to create earthen defenses, covered by soil dug out of deep trenches. Fields surrounding the town were cleared of trees and the earth mounded up and pitted with more trenches. Grand mansion and humble tavern alike were at the mercy of the invading force. The town was overrun with officers quartering in the finer homes, while an encampment of soldiers and their followers arose within and around the village. The grand terraced gardens of the Elder Secretary Nelson's estate, which ran down the bluffs to the river, were shoveled over into fortifications, as Cornwallis made himself a guest at that home. A month and a half later, instead of greeting naval ships from New York, Cornwallis had to order all of his forces to withdraw behind those fortifications and trenches to man their artillery and prepare for a siege.

Generals Washington and Rochambeau, acting on the intelligence of Cornwallis's position at Yorktown, a port on an unprotected peninsula, used their advantage of the French navy to block an escape by sea and marched their forces south to surround the British and lay siege to their position. The allied armies arrived outside of Yorktown with a force of over eighteen thousand. They too began gouging up the fields, throwing up earthen fortifications and digging trenches to support the arriving artillery. On October 9, 1781, the allies opened fire on the British, their larger siege cannons bombarding the town nonstop for eight days and nights. Most of the structures in Yorktown were destroyed and the surrounding landscape of fields cratered by impact explosions.

On October 17, outnumbered, outgunned and overwhelmed by bad luck, General Cornwallis requested General Washington's terms for surrender. Representatives of the British, the Americans and the French met at the abandoned home of Augustine Moore to finalize the Articles of Capitulation. On October 19, with the articles signed, the British marched to a field outside of Yorktown to lay down their weapons. With the formalities of surrender over, it was now General Washington's duty to inform Congress of the results of his campaign.

I

Centennial

"Awe and Disappointment"

Lieutenant Colonel Tench Tilghman, aide-de-camp to General George Washington, was almost arrested for disturbing the peace on the streets of Philadelphia as he sought to awaken Thomas McKean, president of Congress, in the dark hours of October 23, 1781. Entrusted by Washington with the surrender documents, Tilghman had departed the battlefield of Yorktown on the day of the British capitulation, October 19. He traveled day and night, by boat up the Chesapeake and on horseback inland. The dispatches he carried for Congress detailed the allied victory over the British and the terms extracted. During Tilghman's late-night exchange with McKean, the town watchman who had sought to arrest the messenger for his intrusive efforts to wake the house immediately began to spread the news with the "greatest rapidity through the city." Forgoing his customary announcements of the hour, the watchman now proclaimed, "Cornwallis is taken," throughout the town. Before morning, all of Philadelphia was illuminated, and bells rang in celebration.[1] The next span of days saw church services, bell and artillery salutes, fireworks, raucous celebrations and vandalism that terrified the community of Loyalist residents.[2]

On the morning of October 24, Congress met to read the dispatches from General Washington, give congratulatory speeches and form committees to construct the proper mode of communicating the thanks of the United States to the principles. Resolutions were put forth for an official day of thanksgiving to be observed on December 13, which would coincide with the Church of St. Mary's Te Deum and King Louis XVI's order to General

Currier & Ives, "Cornwallis is taken!" 1876. *Library of Congress*.

Rochambeau's army to sing a Te Deum for the victory. On October 29, a committee issued resolutions offering the thanks of Congress to all the principles—Washington, Lafayette, Rochambeau, De Grasse, their staffs and soldiers—along with the distribution of war trophies. For Lieutenant Colonel Tilghman's service, Congress awarded him a horse and an elegant sword, "in testimony of their high opinion of his merit and ability." Among all the official resolutions of praise, thanks and gifts, Congress saw fit to memorialize this event in the newborn nation's history:

> **Resolved, That the United States, in Congress assembled, will cause to be erected, at York, in Virginia, a* marble column, *adorned with emblems of the alliance between the United States and His Most Christian Majesty, and inscribed with a succinct narrative of the surrender of Earl Cornwallis to His Excellency General Washington, commander-in-chief of the combined forces of America and France, to His Excellency the Count de Rochambeau, commanding the auxiliary troops of His Most Christian Majesty in America, and to His Excellency the Count de Grasse, commanding-in-chief the naval army of France in Chesapeake.*[3]

A monument to the alliance and victory at Yorktown. What a wonderful way for a new nation to adorn itself. This was precisely the sentiment of Benjamin Franklin, who was in France at this time. He had been contemplating the minting of a commemorative medal honoring the events of 1776 and the 1777 victory at Saratoga, which had so impressed the French it gained their public support for the American cause. When Franklin received correspondence from Robert R. Livingston, secretary for foreign affairs, detailing the capitulation of Yorktown by the British and Congress's resolution for erecting a commemorative pillar there, it was only natural to incorporate the 1781 date into his medal. Livingston was tasked by Congress to prepare a sketch for the memorial column. His November 1781 correspondence with the French ambassador, Chevalier de la Luzerne, alludes to the chief purpose of the monument, a commemoration of the alliance. Luzerne wrote to Livingston:

> *I have no doubt that they will be most agreeable to his Majesty, and that he will learn with pleasure that the remembrance of the success obtained by the allied armies is to be preserved by a column on which a relation of this event will be inscribed and mention made of alliance. I shall be glad before any further resolutions are taken on the subject to communicate to you some ideas relative to the monument. It is so honorable to the two nations to perpetuate this remembrance of their union that we ought to be mutually desirous of giving it all the solidity and durability of which the works of man are susceptible.*[4]

But there was no further discussion of a monument as the year ended.

Franklin was asked to assist Livingston in producing a sketch and rough estimate for the monument to put before Congress for consideration. In March 1782, Franklin wrote to Livingston that he would endeavor to procure a sketch for the project and shared his idea of a medal. Franklin believed in commemoratives like those of the old empires, which portray a nation's character through classical Greco-Roman symbolism. He wished to depict the young nation as an infant Hercules watched over by a goddess (France) repelling an attacking lion (England). In May 1782, Livingston responded; he was "charmed" with the idea and design of the medal. Replying in August 1782, Franklin wrote that Livingston's approval of the medal gave him encouragement to have it struck. He then requested more information about the desired monument for Yorktown:

> *I wish you would acquaint me with what kind of a monument at York the emblems required are to be fixed on—whether an obelisk or a column, its dimensions, whether any part of it is to be marble, and the emblem carved on it, and whether the work is to be executed by the excellent artists in that way which Paris affords, and if so, to what expense they are to be limited.*

This was the last reference to the Yorktown monument between these two. In 1783, Franklin was concerned with pressing affairs of state, securing treaties and the diplomacy of peace negotiations. He pursued the creation and minting of his "Libertas Americana" medal all at his own expense, gifting them to kings and ambassadors with whom he courted favor. He sent silver, copper and bronze specimens to members of Congress, soliciting their approval. In that year, Livingston resigned his post, and Franklin sought to return home once Thomas Jefferson was settled in as the new country's representative. Franklin was deeply entwined in domestic affairs of state, writing constitutions and such, and Livingston's successor seems not to have taken up the project. With no funds in the treasury for such efforts, the monument would have to wait.

Congress did not follow up on its 1781 resolution. The forming of a national government took precedence, what with writing constitutions and Federalist debates, and budgeting for national monuments moved to the bottom of the list. Only when there was strong public sentiment and vocal outcry were such projects taken on, usually by local authorities and communities. In 1783, Congress resolved to have an equestrian statue of George Washington placed at the residence of Congress to commemorate his role in the war, yet by 1791, they had only proposals. The apathy toward financing monuments at this time can be summed up by the comments of John Jay: "It is only while he lives [Washington] that we can have the satisfaction of offering fruits of gratitude and affection to his enjoyment; posterity can have only the expensive pleasure of strewing flowers on his grave."[5]

Through the first decade after the glorious events at Yorktown, states and cities commissioned statues and monuments to their citizen heroes of the Revolution, and while Yorktown was celebrated in oratory, the place itself languished as a casualty of war, an open wound on the landscape. Like Jamestown before it, Yorktown was fading into the origin story of America; its colonial prominence fell into the ashes from which the reborn independent nation arose. The attention of the country focused on those northern cities where government and, with it, commerce and population, were growing. In Yorktown, there was no talk of monuments or

MEDAL STRUCK BY BENJAMIN FRANKLIN IN FRANCE

In commemoration of the Victories at Saratoga and at Yorktown, 1777 and 1781

Illustration of Benjamin Franklin's Medal, Libertas Americana, *Yorktown Centennial Handbook: Historical and Topographical Guide*, 1881. *Library of Congress.*

commemorations; there were no preservation societies yet demanding that the battlefields and town were sacred and hallowed ground, that this place should be a pilgrimage for all patriots who give thanks for their liberty. Yorktown was a ruin; its sparse and scattered, mostly rural population along the riverbanks did not create the kind of clamor that got attention from those in leadership. Perhaps a reason the 1781 resolution was not acted on at the time is that the residents of Yorktown were beseeching their governor and Congress for aid in repairing the damage the war had caused, not trying to memorialize it. Earthworks, trenches, ordnance and structures thrown up by both armies during the battle remained. The litter of the French quartering during their winter camp and the militia's occupation that followed in the first years after the battle were yet to be dealt with. The residents petitioned to no avail for funds and labor. They wanted the fortifications leveled, the earthworks flattened and the trenches filled so that they could resume their peaceful occupations.[6] No politician would dare bring up financing a monument in a place where the citizens were seeking damages in their county court to redress their losses at the hands of the British troops.[7]

> *Or that they ought to bear at their very doors Mounds of Earth which prevent a free circulation of the Air, and Ditches of stagnant putred* [sic] *water.*[8]

Inhabitants and local officials sought aid for the redevelopment of their town, yet opportunities for using the still-standing Continental Army or a conscripted, enslaved labor force were turned down for fear the defenses would be needed should the British return. When that fear passed, the county magistrates still refused, citing insufficient barracks and supplies for the needed men.

The idea of a grand monument at Yorktown had slipped the minds of those in the General Assembly. Congress refused all requests for money and aid for the town, explaining that other sites had leveled their fortifications without the help of the central government and it did not have the finances to give.[9] Other than petitions to officials, the next few years saw no proactive efforts by the citizens to change their condition. There was a successful effort made to clear the port of the hazards of vessels sunk during the battle so the shipping trade could resume. It would be those returning merchants who found a profit in the battlefield as they dug up the remnants of over fifteen thousand artillery rounds fired during the siege, embedded in the trenches and hills, to ship up north to sell for scrap iron.[10]

Notable European travelers on grand explorations of America passed through Yorktown as they toured the landscapes and critiqued the progress and opportunities of the new nation. One such personage was the French Duke De La Rochefoucault-Liancourt. Traveling North America and documenting sites and histories in his journals of 1796, the duke commented on the state of Yorktown and its lack of a promised monument:

> *The Monument is not even yet begun. Such negligence is inconceivable, shameful, and unaccountable. The present disposition of the American government toward England does not admit of a supposition that they have at this time any thought of erecting that monument.*[11]

In 1798, when artist and architect Benjamin Latrobe visited Yorktown during a tour of Virginia, he found a town that looked as if the battle had ended the day before. Here were the cannon-riddled remains of some fine brick homes like that of Secretary Nelson, which Latrobe sketched and painted. The once terraced gardens that stretched to the river had been turned under into defensive walls and trenches, creating a monochrome palate of the landscape around the relic. Latrobe found it hard to compose something "picturesque."[12] While the scenery did not inspire him, the hospitality of the people and meals of fish and the York's famous oysters at

"View at Little York in Virginia, by Benjamin Henry Latrobe," *An Essay on Landscape, Explained in Tinted Drawings, 1798–1799. The Library of Virginia.*

the local tavern left him with some empathy for the area trying to recover from war, neglect and bad luck.

By the turn of the nineteenth century, twenty-plus years since the great battle, Yorktown had not recovered, to the bitter disappointment of those who knew it in better days. A town that once overshadowed the capitol at Williamsburg in fashion and population, that supplanted Jamestown as a port of exchange and commerce, now tried vainly to keep up appearances. The multiple brick mansions of the Nelson and Lightfoot families still showed the scars of the siege, and the remaining buildings had been somewhat shabbily restored. Yet the only tribute to Yorktown's place in history were four poplar trees planted in a square by William, the grandson of Thomas Nelson Jr., to mark the spot of the sword surrender ceremony. The once commercial waterfront had become an urban slum, refuge for the poorest in the town, whose homes and land had been completely sacrificed to the glory of 1781. These were the people who would again suffer during a war with the British, as the War of 1812 left its mark on Yorktown. On the night of June 12, 1813, the inhabitants of the Yorktown waterfront witnessed the British attack and capture of the American cutter *Surveyor* anchored across the river at Gloucester Point. As the British blockaded the Chesapeake, the residents of Yorktown lived in fear of another siege of their town or mischief from British sympathizers.[13] They believed those fears realized on the afternoon of March 3, 1814, when a fire swept through the wooden shacks and warehouses of the waterfront, climbing up and over the bluff to the main, consuming many of the buildings there, including "the county Courthouse, the Church and the spacious dwelling of the late President Nelson."[14]

Little investment was made to rebuild what was lost, other than the courthouse in 1818. Of all the grand brick mansions built by the Nelson families, now only the 1730s original, built by the patriarch, "Scotch Tom," still stood. Home to the Revolutionary Patriot Thomas Nelson Jr. and his descendants, it was the closest thing to a monument in Yorktown.

Yorktown languished for another ten years as opportunities and hopes of redevelopment faded. It was always on the edge of success, only to come up short. The age of steamer ships came in, and the beautiful York River could not match the commercial opportunities of the James or Potomac Rivers. The York's deep draft ended at West Point, and the Pamunkey and Mattaponi tributaries did not lead to centers of population and trade like Richmond and Washington. The once famed port of Yorktown served no mass trade and was now only a curious side trip for cruising vessels.

The year 1824, however, would push Yorktown back into the national spotlight and consciousness. A living hero of the American Revolution, Marie-Joseph Paul Yves Roch Gilbert du Motier, Marquis de La Fayette—or simply and affectionately, "Lafayette"—returned to America as the "Nation's Guest." One after another, northern cities lavished Lafayette with celebrations, spectacles and entertainments in his honor. Lafayette was treated to tours of the sights where he had battled and helped America win independence. In August of that year, Virginia also extended an invitation to Lafayette to visit the site of his triumph on the forty-third anniversary of the Battle of Yorktown on October 19.

The task of creating and coordinating a suitable production to honor such a legendary, if not worshipped personality, as Lafayette, fell to legislator Robert G. Scott of Richmond. He had twenty-five days and no funds to make it happen. The state's executive could not constitutionally take funds from the treasury for such an event until the legislature could meet and allocate such funds. Scott received personal donations from various civic and political persons until funds could be deducted from the treasury.[15] Yorktown stood completely inadequate for such an event, with no modern infrastructure or resources to accommodate the anticipated crowds. Still not a picturesque scene, with buildings still scarred by war and fire, it was feared Yorktown's event would fall far short of the those of its northern neighbors and disgrace Virginia's genteel image. The town lacked a cultural center, monuments or square to center the event, so the scarred grounds of the historic battle would be the theme of the celebration. Scott coordinated with local committees and the state and local military to give Yorktown a quick facelift and staging with furnishings and necessities acquired from neighboring locales. The battlefields and eroded earthworks were cleared of overgrowth in order to set a stage for ceremony and pageantry. On the field, a temporary monument of sorts was erected for the occasion, a triumphal arch similar to others erected in the cities though which Lafayette was paraded.

> *The arch is 45 feet in height, surmounted by a large eagle, in imitation of the one at St. Stephen's chapel at Rome, cut out of wood and painted to imitate sculptured marble. The whole front is painted of a light brownish stone color for the ground. The arch has thirteen key stones, to appearance of white marble, with a star in relief on each, corresponding in number with the thirteen original states of the union. On each side of the basement story is represented the fasces, emblematical of unity, and implements of war. The entablature is supported by four columns of pilasters, in imitation of white marble; between the pilasters are placed two figures, the one representing Justice, the other, Liberty trampling upon Tyranny; over these are placed the names "Hamilton" and "Laurens." Over the arch are two figures of Fame, and the name of La Fayette, in large letters, fills the top of the entablature, immediately under the eagle.*[16]

Two wooden obelisks seventy-six feet high, painted to look like stone and covered with various ornaments and emblems of war and victory, were also placed on the field, one at the site of the British Redoubt No. 9 bearing the names of Viomenil, Dumat, Dupont and De Noailles, with appropriate ornaments consisting of Fame, Valor, Prudence, Victory and emblems of elegance and taste. The second was placed near Nelson's poplar trees at the site of the surrender of the sword. It was inscribed with Washington's name on the front; to the west, "First in War"; to the south, "First in Peace"; and to the east, "First in the Hearts of his Countrymen." Over the inscriptions were figures of History, War, Peace and Agriculture. On the shaft of the obelisk were inscribed the names of Nelson, Rochambeau, St. Simon and De Grasse.[17] The field, with its monuments and pageants, was the focus of attention during the day, while dinner and dancing under the preserved tent of George Washington, brought down from Mount Vernon for the occasion, occupied the night.

"An Example of the Triumphal Arches Erected in the Cities of Lafayette's Tour." Printed in the September 8, 1824 edition of *The Casket* literary magazine. *The collection of Lafayette College.*

The throngs that attended the three-day event were on their own for accommodations, the military set up its own camps and the dignitaries who attended were housed in what few comfortable buildings were available. Lafayette was guest of William Nelson and spent two nights in the old home of Thomas Nelson Jr., the man he had stood beside in battle so many years ago. The house still bore the scars as an artillery target offered up by Nelson to flush out Cornwallis. Once the speeches, ceremonies, entertainments and dinners were over, Lafayette departed, continuing on his grand tour toward Williamsburg and Richmond. The crowds followed after, receding from Yorktown like the tide, leaving its faux monuments, litter and whitewash to fade with the autumn rains. Yorktown's rough and sparse appearance had amused attendees, giving the quaint ambience of being frozen in time with the field of battle, allowing minds to envision heroic deeds on the plain. This was an event that drew attention to preservation of the sacred field—that bane of the residents, who continually sought to level and fill in, would become an object of opportunity as the age of "historic tourism" took hold in America.

The publicity of Lafayette's tour and the fading away of those living connections to glory gave rise to the interest of a collective nationalism. The growing historical societies formed from the social associations of Virginia's "First Families," as well as the academic historian groups of Massachusetts and Connecticut, renewed interest in establishing a monument at Yorktown, regularly bringing it up in their meetings and writing congressional officials. In 1834 and again in 1836, Congress referred the resolution of a monument to a select committee, which stalled and was lost among the subjects of appropriation law.[18]

A generation after the great battle, Yorktown hosted occasional travelers who, versed in their nation's history, sought a physical connection to those events of the past. Some came for the entertainment of tourism, others to validate and document the national memory. Both groups encountered the town with the same mix of stirring patriotic awe and critical commentary on the want of modern accommodations and comfort. In the first fifty years of the nineteenth century, visitors to Yorktown could explore the very scars of the battle, following documented history, or be regaled with secondhand accounts by residents like Robert Anderson, who had many recovered artifacts and often acted as an area guide. In this period, many stories were lost and some created by visiting self-styled historians who confused the house and life of Secretary Thomas Nelson with that of his nephew Governor and General Thomas Nelson Jr., eschewing history books even to this very day. Visitors who engaged local residents were treated to stories and legends presented as facts regarding landmarks and points of interest like Cornwallis's Cave and the Moore House.[19]

Benson J. Lossing, in his thorough *Pictorial Field-Book of the Revolution*, published after his 1848 visit, sought to present as true as possible

"Centennial—Characters and Incidents of the Event." *From* Frank Leslie's Illustrated Newspaper, *November 5, 1881.*

the history and the environs of Yorktown. Filled with illustrations and footnotes, it chronicled not only the factual history but also his observations of the landscape. Escorted through the sites by William Nelson, grandson of the famed Thomas, Lossing recorded the subject of Yorktown's lack of monuments:

> *It is the opinion of Mr. Nelson and other intelligent gentlemen at Yorktown, that the large field, noted as the spot on the map…is the locality where the captive soldiers laid down their arms, and where the marble column, ordered by Congress, should be erected.*

Lossing then noted:

> *The marble for this column, like many other monuments ordered by the Continental Congress is yet in the quarry.*[20]

Yorktown had become America's own Brigadoon, rising out of the mists of memory to live for a brief moment, sought out and found only by those who knew it was there. October 19 had become an observance day of toasts and banquets for the societies of the northern academics. In Virginia, the local military regiments and patriotic societies had sanctified the day in the years since Lafayette's visit. As the country moved ever closer to the coming conflict tearing apart the Union, Virginia's state pride took action to memorialize Yorktown, no longer waiting for the long promised congressional monument. During the 1860 October observance, with the approval of the governor, a monument was installed by the attending militia companies. Near the vicinity of Nelson's poplar trees and a pile of stones reported to have been ballast from Lafayette's ship, a marble column was finally raised. Provided by the Marble Yard of John W. Davies

Present Appearance of the British Works at Yorktown.[1]

Illustration of earthworks remaining at Yorktown. *The Pictorial Field-Book of the Revolution*, vol. 2. *Benson J. Lossing.*

in Richmond,[21] the thirteen-foot white marble shaft sat atop two blocks of James River granite and was inscribed:

> *Erected the 19th day of October, 1860, by the regimental and company officers of the Twenty-first Regiment of Virginia militia of Gloucester County, and of the volunteer company attached hereto, to mark the spot of the surrender of Cornwallis' sword on the 19th of October, 1781.*

Perhaps as a foreshadowing of things to come, due to stormy weather, the monument could not be installed on the nineteenth, and was delayed until the twenty-ninth.[22] Unfortunately, this monument would not stand and proclaim Yorktown's fame through the ages; it became victim to the cultural atrocities of war committed by both sides. First, it was the Confederate troops that fortified Yorktown, throwing up their own defensive works over the eroding siege landscape of the prior war. In their admiration and awe of the historic place they were in, the soldiers sought relics of that time, chipping pieces of the marble for mementos, "the marble industriously fashioned into venerating tokens of biblical form for distant mothers and sisters, and into expensive emblems for anxious sweethearts."[23]

By the time the Union army was set to lay siege to the town in May 1862, half of the monument had disappeared. When the Union troops occupied Yorktown later that month, it was supposed that the rest of the monument had been carried off by Southerners to keep it from falling into Yankee hands. Only the granite base remained, too heavy to carry off. It, too, fell prey to the hammers of Union relic hunters.

The Union would also aid in the monument's disappearance by establishing a Federal cemetery in the area where the monument had stood. During the war and after, Union dead were relocated from other hasty burials at battle sites around the area and reinterred at Yorktown. The layout of interments and landscaping of the area destroyed and obscure the location of Nelson's trees and that first monument. With no known photographs or sketches, only the scarce few letters and diary pages of soldiers who saw it can attest to its existence.[24]

The years following the Civil War found Yorktown residents in a condition that was familiar. The village was worn down by a military occupation, the upheaval of the landscape, destruction and vandalism, and now the residents perceived oppressive indignities of having lands confiscated not only for a Federal cemetery honoring the Union dead, but also a newly established community of contraband (the formerly enslaved). The war's end and

Above: Photograph of Yorktown National Cemetery from inside looking toward the lodge. *Records of the Office of the Quartermaster General, National Archives*.

Left: Colossal hand and torch, "Liberty." Pennsylvania, Philadelphia, circa 1876. *Library of Congress*.

destruction of the South's culture left a large void in the ego and identity of half the nation as it tried to close the wounds and be made whole again. Those who sought hope for "a more perfect union," to foster a rekindled national identity, looked toward the coming anniversaries that would take place throughout the 1870s as America neared its one hundredth birthday.

The 1875 centennial of the Bunker Hill battle and the 1876 Exposition in Philadelphia, where the colossal arm and torch of the unfinished Statue of Liberty was on display, inspired a movement led by the editor of the *Norfolk Virginian*, M. Glennan, Esq. The goal to secure a "National Celebration of the Centennial of the Surrender of Lord Cornwallis at Yorktown and the erection of the monument in compliance with the resolution of the Continental Congress of 1781." Support for the event would be welcomed by the president of the Virginia Historical Society, joined by the resolutions of other historical societies to advocate for a national decree. Influential newspapers of the day began to take up the cause, and the support of the national press followed. A mass meeting of the citizens and sponsors was held in Yorktown, where arrangements were made for the preliminary celebrations of '79 and '80 in anticipation of the event of '81.[25]

A meeting of the states' governors was held in Philadelphia on October 18, 1879, in which all present enthusiastically endorsed the proposition and appointed commissioners in each state to create interest in the matter. A meeting of the local Yorktown Centennial Association resolved to seek a national observance of the Yorktown Centennial and that Congress should give "practical effect" to the 1781 monument resolution, ending with:

> *That the Hon. John Goode, Representative of the Congressional district in Virginia, which embraces within its bounds the historic spot made famous by the event of 19th October, 1781, is hereby requested to bring the subject before the National Legislature at its next session, and urge the prompt and speedy fulfillment of the Nation's pledge made nearly a century ago.*[26]

At the opening of Congress, the resolutions were presented by the Honorable John Goode, a committee was organized and a bill promptly recorded requesting an appropriation of $100,000 for the erection of the monument and $20,000 to contribute to the celebration of the centennial, followed by an additional $20,000 appropriation.

> * *AN ACT to carry into effect the resolution of Congress, adopted on the twenty-ninth of October, seventeen hundred and eighty-one, in regard*

to a monumental column, at Yorktown, Virginia, and for other purposes. Approved, June 7, 1880[27]

Huzzah!

The project, now under the jurisdiction of the War Department, was assigned to the Corps of Engineers to implement under the supervision of Lieutenant Colonel William Price Craighill.

Later to become brigadier general and an icon of the Army Corps of Engineers, LIEUTENANT COLONEL WILLIAM PRICE CRAIGHILL was a Virginian who served in the Union army, building fortifications and defensive lines. After the war, he headed the Engineer Office in Baltimore overseeing river and harbor work throughout the Chesapeake Bay. During the centennial festivities, he organized and constructed all the needed infrastructure. Craighill laid out arrangements for sanitation, water supply and presentation of encampments that would become a standard for future maneuvers. He was assigned to procure and prepare the site for the monument, overseeing all details of its construction through completion.

Secretary of War Alexander Ramsey appointed a commission of artists to recommend a suitable monument design, and the commission then appointed itself for the production of the project. The commission consisted of three men who during their collective careers were responsible for epic and timeless works that define the American character. These men were peers and collaborators on various projects, and at the time of the centennial, all three had other projects in production moving apace with the growing and expanding country. J.Q.A. Ward was working on a monument to the late President Garfield, R.M. Hunt was designing the pedestal for the Statue of Liberty and Henry Van Brunt was to take on a commission from the railroad to build its grand terminal stations in the West. For this group of esteemed professionals, the Yorktown Monument, far away from the centers of culture, growing industry and population, seems to have been somewhat of a side project.

Brigadier General William Price Craighill. *Norfolk District Public Affairs, U.S. Army Corps of Engineers.*

JOHN QUINCY ADAMS WARD is known as the "Dean of American Sculpture." He was a

Left: J.Q.A. Ward, standing at fence. *Library of Congress.*

Right: Henry Van Brunt. *The Reading Room/Alamy Stock Photo.*

renowned classical sculptor whose public and private commissions dotted the cultural landscapes of New York; Washington, D.C.; and Boston. Naturalism was the dominant feature of his art, and he was famed for his naturalistic portraiture. As Ward was an advocate and creator of America's own artistic style, his public works of heroic citizens and representations of the human spirit made him a perfect choice to create a fitting tribute to the subject of the Revolution's victory and pay homage to an important ally. He provided the symbolic decorative elements as well as the crowning figure for the proposed column.

HENRY VAN BRUNT was a nationally known architect based in Boston with the affiliation of Harvard and the Massachusetts Institute of Technology. His firm designed the finer homes of society and built impressive public buildings and private monuments. Van Brunt later moved his firm west to Kansas City, where he would influence the architecture of the Midwest with his railroad terminal commissions. A prolific essayist on the science and philosophy of architecture, he provided the "math" of the column, structural design calculations for its erection and stability.

Richard Morris Hunt, 1895. *Library of Congress.*

A highly respected architect and artist, RICHARD MORRIS HUNT designed buildings that combined history, aesthetics and modern technology. He was a founder who shaped and professionalized architectural practice and education in the United States. Hunt was much sought out by many of the Gilded Age luminaries to create their celebrated manors and mansions such as Vanderbilt's Biltmore Estate in North Carolina. He also lent his talents to the design of public works and monuments. Hunt was designing the pedestal for the Statue of Liberty in New York when he joined the Yorktown commission. His task was to create the base for the column, which would enshrine the narratives of the commemoration. As chairman of the commission, he directed the procurements and administration of the project.

On December 2, 1880, the commission sent its model to the war office for approval.

> *The model forwarded is five feet and a half high. It consists of a Corinthian column and capital designed by Mr. Hunt, surmounted with a figure, bearing a round of feathers in high relief. For the statue at the top Mr. Ward submits four figures of liberty and victory for selection. In recesses in the sides of the pedestal, from which the column springs, are in front the coats of arms of France and the United States, side by side, on the right, naval; and on the left, army attributes; beyond are emblems of peace. On a cylinder above are thirteen female figures in alto relief, representing the original colonies, hand joined to hand; on a legend "One Country, One Destiny, One Constitution." There are numerous other emblematic and architectural ornaments.*[28]

An extract from the report of the commission of artists explains the emblematic significance of the monument:

> *From the point of view of sentiment, this monument is intended to convey, in architectural language, the idea, set forth in the dedicatory inscription, that, by the victory at Yorktown, the independence of the United States of America was achieved, or brought to final accomplishment.*

Cabinet card photo of monument model, 1881. *Author's collection.*

"Study for Victory, from the sketchbook of J.Q.A. Ward," circa 1860. *The Metropolitan Museum of Art Collection API.*

The four sides of the base contain, first, an inscription dedicating the monument as a memorial of the victory; second, an inscription presenting a succinct narrative of the siege, prepared in accordance with the original archives in the Department of State; third, the treaty of alliance with the King of France; and, fourth, the treaty of peace with the King of England. In the pediments over these four sides, respectively, are presented, carved in relief, first, emblems of nationality; second, emblems of war; third, emblems of the alliance; and fourth, emblems of peace.

The base is thus devoted to the historical statement; it explains the subsequent incidents of the monumental composition, which are intended solely to appeal to the imagination. The immediate result of the historical events written upon the base was the happy establishment of a national union of thirteen youthful, free and independent States. To celebrate this joyful union the sculptor has represented upon the circular podium, which arises from the base, a solemn dance of thirteen typical female figures,

> *hand-in-hand, encircling the drum, which bears upon a belt beneath their feet the word "One country, one constitution, one destiny." It is a symbol of the birth of freedom.*
>
> *The column which springs from this podium may be accepted as the symbol of greatness and prosperity of the nation after a century of various experience, when thirty-eight free and independent States are shining together in mighty constellation. It is the triumphant sign of the fulfilment of the promise—an expression of the strength and beauty of the Union; but the powerful nation does not forget the remote beginning of its prosperity, and, in the midst of its shining stars, bears aloft the shield of Yorktown covering the branch of peace.*
>
> *As the existence of the nation is a proof of the possibility of a government of the people by the people for the people, the column, thus adorned, culminates with Liberty herself, star-crowned, and welcoming the people of all nations to share equally with us the fruits of our peace and prosperity.*[29]

The dimensions of the overall monument according to the drawings and model were as follows:

> *Base, 25 feet 8 inches.*
> *Podium, 14 feet 4 inches.*
> *Shaft, 35 feet 1 inch.*
> *Capital, 5 feet 9 inches.*
> *Pedestal, 3 feet 9 inches.*
> *Figure, 11 feet 4 inches.*

For a total height of 95 feet, 6 inches, from the surface of the ground to the top of the figure, the planned base would cover a surface area of 945.56 feet.[30] The height of the figure would later be altered to 13 feet.

The model was approved by the end of December 1880, and with funding in place and the centennial plans in coordination, the task fell to Lieutenant Colonel Craighill to prepare for the cornerstone ceremony, which would take place during the festivities in October 1881. Craighill had piers and wharves constructed that would accommodate not only the crowds that would

THE YORKTOWN MONUMENT

(FROM THE ACCEPTED MODEL)

"Sketch of the Accepted Model by the Artist Commission, 1881." *Yorktown Centennial Handbook: Historical and Topographical Guide. Library of Congress.*

arrive for the celebration but also the construction materials and equipment that would be arriving over the coming years for the monument project. Surveys were conducted of all the environs of Yorktown to provide for the incoming military camps and to seek out a suitable site for the monument.

During the planning years, the Yorktown Centennial Association, purchased the Temple Farm, consisting of five hundred acres, and the historic Moore House, site of the 1781 surrender negotiations. This property it proposed to donate to the U.S. government to be converted into a park named for the beloved Lafayette, "In honor of the illustrious hero, whose unselfish devotion to liberty prompted him to come to the assistance of the struggling colonies, and whose name is inseparably associated with the final commemoration of our Independence at Yorktown."[31]

In June 1881, a survey was made of fifteen acres just inside the gate to Temple Farm on the riverbank, which the Centennial Association proposed to donate as a site for the monument. The association hoped business development and the railroad would follow the centennial investments; however, in July another site on the edge of town was chosen.[32] Lafayette Park would not be established, and the mortal wounding of President Garfield on July 2 distracted the public's attention from the fundraising effort. The association, deep in debt and controversy, later had to give up the title to the property.[33]

On July 6, the U.S. government purchased town lots from W.W. Old and H.C. Camble, special commissioners representing part of the estate of Robert Anderson, which had encompassed all of Secretary Nelson's estate lot, among others. The purchase price was $1,000, plus the fees for title research and recording, for a sum total of $1,520.24. Situated on a hill rising above the water, the lot at the edge of the town afforded an uninterrupted view of the river's course. The site was covered with fieldworks erected by the Confederate forces under General John Magruder; these were leveled off, and preparations began on the monument's foundation. None of the materials needed to start construction, except sand, was available near Yorktown, and that had to be hauled from a distance. The need for a coordinator was solved when E.H. Kirlin was brought in to be the site overseer. He had been previously engaged constructing the dams and locks on the Great Kanawha River project.

> *A pit was sunk near the exact spot chosen for the Monument to stand upon. The soil to a depth of 7 feet was found to consist of fine sand in the proportion of two-thirds, the remaining third being red clay. At a depth of*

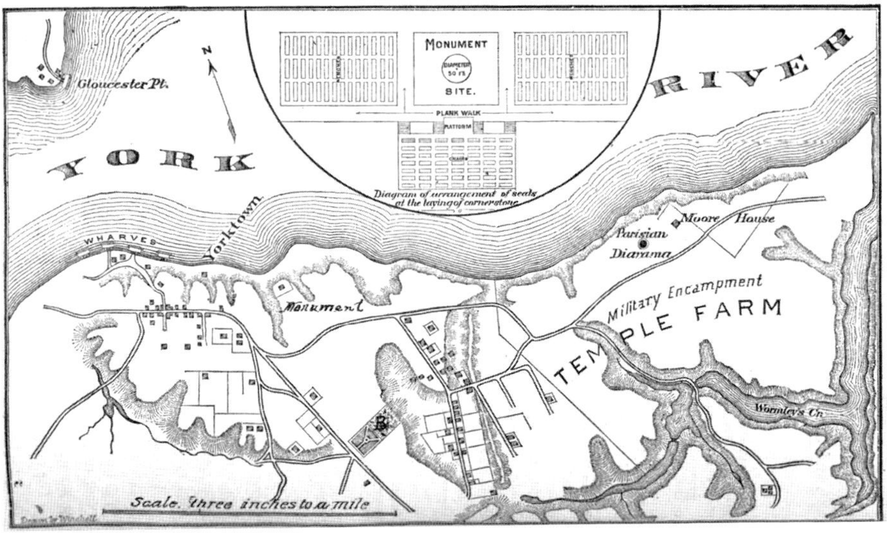

"Map of the Centennial Grounds and Monument Site," from *Yorktown: a Compendious Account of the Campaign, and the Celebration of the Centennial*, 1882. *Library of Congress.*

15 or 20 feet, as shown in lateral ravines, was found a pure red clay over a soft conglomerate of shells and sandstone. It was determined, in accordance with the liberty granted by your letter of instructions, to make a foundations of concrete. The broken stone was procured in Richmond, by purchase in open market, as time was too short to allow of advertising for proposals, &c. The stone came from the same quarries which have furnished so much of the material for the new State, War, and Navy Departments in Washington. The cement was brought in from Baltimore. The bottom of the base of the Monument was fixed by the commission of artists as a square, with sides of 30 feet, and receding in steps to a square whose sides are about 20 feet each. The foundations of concrete were made 6 feet deep, square in plan, 41 feet on the side at bottom, 31½ feet, on the sides at tops, and amounting to 316½ cubic yards, including the corner-stone.

The corner-stone was in two parts, the principal piece being 4½ feet long, 4 feet wide, and 2½ feet deep, covered by a cap-stone of the same length and breadth, and 1 foot thick. The hole in the lower stone, of which the dimensions were fixed by the Masons to contain a copper box, was 2½ feet long, 2 feet wide, and 18 inches deep. The dimensions of the corner-stone were so arranged that the box should have every side of it a thickness of 1 foot of stone. The stone itself was put in so deep in the foundations as to be entirely imbedded in concrete, and to have one foot of concrete over it.[34]

Cornerstone ceremony at the one hundredth anniversary of the Battle of Yorktown, 1881. *USN 900377, National Archives.*

Virginia-sourced granite used in the foundation was sent by tug and barge from Richmond. The material for the cornerstone and the derrick for lowering the cap were furnished at no cost by the Granite Company of Richmond, Colonel R. Snowden Andrew, president.

After the concrete footing and stone foundation were laid, Craighill had a wooden stage platform constructed over it, providing for viewing stands to accommodate the guests, military band and press. An opening in the platform to access the cornerstone and a derrick for lowering the cover completed the stage for the sacred Masonic ceremonies to come.

The Grand Lodge of Virginia conducted the corner stone ceremonies. Grand Master Peyton S. Cole appealed to all lodges for their attendance, and despite the crude and remote locale, one thousand Masons arrived to take part in the grand procession, escorted by the Knights Templar. These groups were quartered in a section of the organized tent city with the military. Grand masters from the thirteen original states took part in the rituals held on October 18. The ceremony began with invocation, oration and hymn. The right worshipful brother grand secretary then read the inscription on the copper box to be placed in the stone:

Corner-stone of a Monument to Commemorate the Surrender of Lord Cornwallis and the forces under his Command, to the American and French Troops at Yorktown, October 19th, 1781.

Laid on the invitation of the Congressional Commission by the Grand Lodge of A.F. & A. Masons of Virginia, on the occasion of the celebration of the 100th anniversary of that event.

The grand secretary then read the list of the contents of the box:

- *one copy of the Holy Bible*
- *copper coin of United States, 1783*
- *copper coin, 1783, Washington and Independence*
- *silver coin of United States, 1776*
- *three metal medals*
- *copper coin of 1787, "Mind your Business"*
- *colonial coin of 1773.*
- *¼ franc*
- *one cent, Canada coin of 1773*
- *one French coin, 1874*
- *$100 Virginia Treasury note of October 1862*
- *$100 Confederate interest-bearing note*
- *copy of program issued by the Commercial Club, Richmond, of the celebration at Yorktown and continued in Richmond*
- *photograph of Confederate Flags combined*
- *Yorktown Centennial Medal*
- *Memorial Schedule of Arrival and Departure of Mails, issued September 26, 1881, Richmond Post Office*
- *copy of* Virginia Real Estate Journal *of October 1881*
- *copy of* Travels of Ego and Alter, *published in 1879*
- *copy of* Methods of Language Teaching, *and copy of Yorktown Centennial volume*
- *copy of "The Yorktown Campaign and the Surrender of Cornwallis, 1781"*
- *copy of the* Warrock-Richardson Almanac *for 1881*
- *copy of charter of Yorktown Centennial Association*
- *By-Laws of South Carolina Commandery No. 1, chartered in 1824*
- *copy of By-Laws, Joppa Lodge No. 40, Richmond*
- *copy of Sketch of Solomon Lodge No. 1; also Copy of By-Laws*
- *copy of By-Laws, Winter Park Lodge No.94, Chesterfield*

- *copy of postal card calling meeting of lodge to consider the Yorktown Centennial, Amity Lodge No. 76, Richmond*
- *a leaf from the Bible on which George Washington was made a Mason; also extracts from Records of Fredericksburg Lodge No. 4, showing his connection with it; also a Roll of Members, 1881*
- *list of names of Yorktown Centennial Chorus and Membership Ticket; also a copy of all the Music to be sung by the Centennial Chorus.*
- *list of officers and members of Amity Lodge No. 76, Richmond, October 1881*
- *Masonic apron worn by the late Reverend Archibald W. Baldwin of Chesterfield County*
- *Copy in MS. Of a work titled "Washington and Lee, with parallel notes," by H.S. Bogart, Savannah, Georgia*
- *copy of proceedings for 1880; also copy of form of diploma on parchment from the Grand Commandery of Knights Templar of Virginia*
- *Copy of Dove's R.A.C. Text-Book, edition 1853; copy of proceedings for 1880; copy of form of diploma on parchment; copy of form of charter on parchment; copy of form of commission to grand representatives; copies of official commissions and dispensations, Grand Chapter of Virginia*
- *copy of first and fourth editions of Dove's Text-Books; copy of proceedings of laying the cornerstone by the Grand Lodge of the Washington Monument, February 22, 1850; copy of unveiling the same, February 22, 1858; copy of proceedings for 1878, containing ceremony of unveiling the monument erected by the Masons of Virginia to memory of Dr. John Dove, who had served as grand secretary from 1836 to 1876; copy of proceedings for 1880; copy of report of proceedings from 1733 to 1822, steel-plate engravings of the grand masters who had presided over the Grand Lodge from 1778 to 1822, also of the late grand secretary; an electrotype of subordinate lodges on parchment, signed by the present grand master; copy of form of diploma on parchment; copy of commission issued to grand representatives; copies of forms of dispensation and other official documents; copy of special committee on Masonic jurisprudence, adopted in 1856; copy of special committee on Free Masonry and the war, adopted in 1864; copy of the program of the ceremony of laying the cornerstone of this monument; copy of the Code of Virginia, edition of 1873; copy of Webster's Dictionary (unabridged); a full set of lodge jewels of silver, contributed by the Grand Lodge of Virginia*

The grand treasurer and grand secretary saw that box was deposited in the prepared place. The grand master of Virginia, with the trowel, stood at the east; the grand master of New York, with the square, on his right; the grand master of Maryland, with the level, at the west; and the grand master of Pennsylvania, with the plumb, at the south side of the stone. The Virginia grand master spread the cement, after which he directed the grand marshal to order the craftsmen to lower the capstone. This was done in three motions: first, lowering the stone a few inches and stopping while the grand honors were given; second, lowering again a few inches and repeating the grand honors; third, lowering to its place and repeating the grand honors. The square, level and plumb were then applied to the stone by their respective bearers and then all returned to their stations. The grand masters of the Grand Lodges of South Carolina, North Carolina, Connecticut, New Hampshire, Rhode Island and Delaware examined the foundation stone and pronounced it true, trusty and duly laid.

Next the grand masters of Massachusetts, North Carolina and Connecticut anointed the stone and offered invocations:

First, the corn of nourishment was poured on the stone: "May the Supreme Architect of the Universe preserve the health and strength of the workmen engaged in the erection of this Monument, protect them from all accidents, and bless and prosper the work of their hands." Second, the wine of refreshment: "May abundant refreshment be showered down upon the people of this our common country, and may the blessings of the Giver of all good things attend their undertakings." Third, the oil of joy and gladness: "May the Supreme Being preserve to the people of this country Peace and harmony, and vouchsafe to them joy and gladness and every blessing."

The grand master of Virginia descended to the stone and gave it three distinctive knocks; he then pronounced the cornerstone of the monument true, trusty and well laid. He then presented "Brother Craighill" the implements of operative Masonry "with the fullest confidence in your skill and ability to erect such a Monument as will perpetuate and add new luster to the established glory, liberality, and patriotism of the people of these United States." Finally, the grand master requested "His Excellency" Chester A. Arthur, president of the United States, to descend and examine the work and, if approved, to receive it from their hands. President Arthur pronounced it well laid and received.[35]

The laying of the cornerstone and the first major event appearance of the recently sworn in President Chester A. Arthur were the high points of the centennial celebrations. Delegations of French and German diplomats and

"View of Centennial Grounds," Centennial Album of Yorktown and of Richmond, VA, 1881. *Author's collection.*

their heroic family descendants were honored during the occasion. Although British delegates were not invited to participate, President Arthur authorized a formal artillery salute to the British flag in response to Queen Victoria's condolences and overtures on the nation's behalf regarding President Garfield's death. This communique was read to the crowd, and the response was a burst of enthusiasm as hands clapped and hats and handkerchiefs waved. In that moment, the symbolism of the monument commemorating the British defeat simply became a record of historical fact, as animosities between the two great nations faded.

Over four days, Yorktown's centennial celebration featured a display of naval power, orations by various luminaries, patriotic poetry, stirring band performances led by a young John Philip Sousa, sundry entertainments, chorus, pyrotechnical displays, military parades, receptions and dances. Attending the military pageants and representing the state of Maryland as a colonel was Oswald Tilghman, wearing one of his ancestor's famed swords.[36]

Illustrations of the military's might and pageantry alongside the crude infrastructure of the town were featured by the popular newspapers of the day. The lack of accommodations and facilities, clouds of dust kicked up by the crowds and local residents portrayed as gouging hucksters and dunces—perpetuating the "Sambo" stereotype of Black residents—were the images and criticisms of the centennial presented to northern readers.[37]

> *As a fizzle in many respects the Yorktown Centennial celebrations will probably take the first prize.*

Criticism was directed at the organizers of the cornerstone ceremony for the inclusion of Confederate relics:

> *The placing of Confederate money, photographs of Confederate flags, etc., under the corner-stone of the Yorktown Monument strikes us as in very bad taste, as much so as would have been the preservation of British money and flags, or the portrait of Benedict Arnold in the same place. The monument is to commemorate the deeds of patriots, not traitors.*[38]

The wave of attendees and participants all swept into Yorktown and, after a few days, receded like the tide. They left behind chaos and litter and took with them a perpetual impression of Yorktown's soaring patriotic awe and critical disappointment.

Now after one hundred years, work could at long last begin on the "The Monument to Alliance and Victory," just as soon as all the governmental red tape could be cleared. After the centennial ceremonies and celebrations were over, the remainder of the foundations were fixed in and the cornerstone covered with concrete. In late October 1881, Craighill wrote to Robert Todd Lincoln, the secretary of war:

> *It is not expected that anything more will be done toward the construction of the Monument until after the cession of jurisdiction over the site by the legislature of Virginia, which will meet, it is understood, in January next....A map of the site and its surroundings will be prepared as soon as other more urgent duties permit."*
>
> *The site was left in the charge of a respectable colored man, who lives in the small, cheap, frame house, about 12 feet square (a single room), near the foundations, used as an office during work on them, and to be so used again when the construction of the Monument begins. He serves without other compensation than the privilege of living in this little house.*[39]

The foundations settled during the winter months while the Virginia legislature worked to approve the cession of jurisdiction over the site.

"The Yorktown Centennial—Military and Naval Reviews." *Harper's Weekly*, October 29, 1881. *Courtesy of the U.S. Naval Art Collection, Washington, D.C.*

"Centennial—Characters and Incidents of the Event." *From* Frank Leslie's Illustrated Newspaper, *November 5, 1881.*

Yorktown was left with a large empty lot for the curious passersby and the occasional livestock to roam, while elsewhere events were proceeding toward the goal of the long-promised monument.

1882

This year started with controversies, as the Congressional Centennial Commission came under fire for its expenditures of excessive personal wining and dining with government funds. Later in the year, the Yorktown Centennial Association was called to court as its creditors pressed for judgment on its assets. The association forfeited its deed to Temple Farm, and the dream of a National Park at Yorktown seemed to fade.

April 22 The deed, act of cession and plat, containing 10.75 acres, are recorded by the clerk of York County.

June 27 The secretary of war issues instructions to proceed with the preparations for the building of the monument.

September 20 The commission of artists is paid $3,000 for the model they submitted and approved in 1881, and these same men are engaged to finish their design and begin contracting for competent persons and materials to complete the work.

October 19 Lieutenant Colonel Craighill is absent in the autumn, being on duty on the Pacific coast. A consultation with him is requested by the chairman of the commission and occurs in early November.

November 27 Specifications and drawings are prepared and proposals for furnishing materials and construction called for by advertisement.

By the end of the year, no construction had taken place on the site.

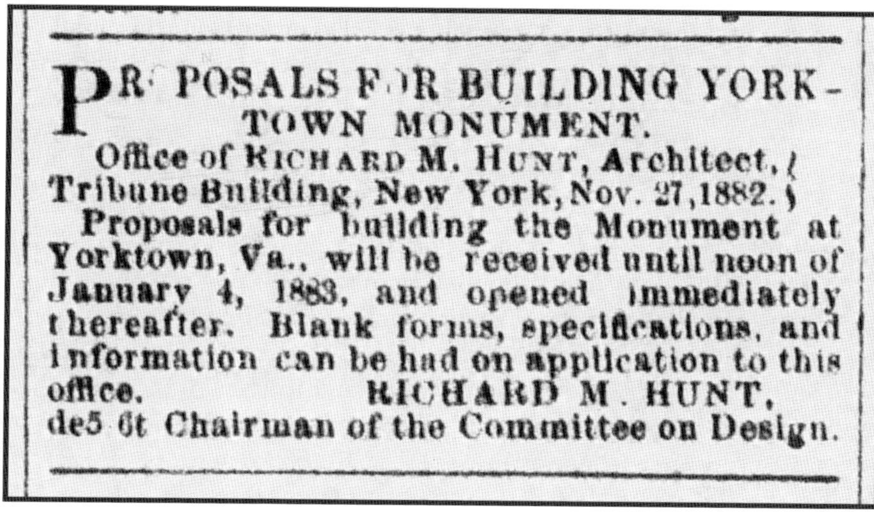

PROPOSALS FOR BUILDING YORK-TOWN MONUMENT.

Office of RICHARD M. HUNT, Architect, Tribune Building, New York, Nov. 27, 1882.

Proposals for building the Monument at Yorktown, Va., will be received until noon of January 4, 1883, and opened immediately thereafter. Blank forms, specifications, and information can be had on application to this office. RICHARD M. HUNT, de5 6t Chairman of the Committee on Design.

Advertisement for contract bids for building the monument, December 6, 1882. *From* the Norfolk Landmark.

1883

January 4 The sealed proposals are opened in the office of Richard Hunt in the presence of Ward, Craighill, the bidders and representatives of the press.

January 11 An abstract of the bids is forwarded to the general of engineers, Brigadier General H.G. Wright.

February 3 Final recommendations as to the award of the contract are made.

February 16 The secretary of war, on the recommendation of the commission of artists, accepts the bid of Hallowell Granite Company on the Kennebec River, Maine, for a total cost of $66,927.

March 9 The necessary papers are sent to the president of Hallowell.

March 30 The contract is finally signed after a delay in certification, due to the absence of the bondsman, tending to a death in the family.

April 10 The contract is approved by the chief of engineers.

August 9 Charles Humphreys takes up a post at Hallowell as inspector and project supervisor; the quarrying and cutting of stone begins.

September An investigation into the stability of the monument's design, in regard to wind pressure, is made by Captain Thomas Turtle.

In the autumn, a detailed survey of the site and the adjacent slopes was made to ensure complete drainage and assured stability. Some distance from the base, a stone was sunk to serve as a survey reference marking 65.944 feet above mean low water.

1884

The Hallowell Company of Maine won the contract to provide the stone for the monument. Hallowell was renowned for the quality of its granite, used by many contractors for cultural public and private buildings. The company was also favored by the commission of artists, who had established the criteria for the stone:

> *Three main qualities of the granite are to be considered in selecting the stone for the monument-strength, durability, and color as to suitableness and permanence....*[40]

> *All the granite* [is] *to be of first quality, light in tone, and even in color, close grained, good texture, free from cracks, seams, flaws, iron marks, discolorations, and defects of every kind, and the dimensions required by the drawings.*[41]

"Stinchfield Quarry near Hallowell Maine," *The Granites of Maine*, Bulletin 313, 1907. *Courtesy of Peggy B. Perazzo.*

The granite would come from Hallowell's Stinchfield Quarry, where the stone was light gray in color with a fine texture, preferred for delicate ornamental work and statuary. This stone also had the property of becoming brighter and whiter as it was exposed to the elements.

The stone was carved at Hallowell by skilled master carvers adhering to the sculptor's models. The monument has three main parts:

BASE | 21 feet, 11.5 inches high, area 30 feet 6.75 inches square on the ground
SCULPTURED PODIUM AND "DRUM" | 21 feet, 7 inches high and 9 feet, 7 inches in diameter
COLUMN | 32 feet 5 inches high and at the base 5 feet, 6 inches in diameter.

The exposed faces of the foundation and base blocks were to be dressed to a smooth surface with point chisels and then finished with fine ten-steel patent hammer work. The four narrative texts were to be of carved, raised and polished lettering with a one-inch projection. In February, cutting began on the twenty-five-ton drum section, at 9 feet, 6 inches in diameter and 8 feet, 10 inches high. The drum was designed in eight pieces—six for the base and two that formed the caryatids (columns in the shape of females).

The derrick to be used for erecting the monument was constructed in Boston by the firm of Cheney & Turnbull—a mast of a single stick 102 feet long and a boom, 98 feet. These were cut from timber in Oregon and sailed around Cape Horn. It was stated that suitable trees could not be found in any other part of the country, which rankled state officials and business leaders, already dismayed by a majority of the contracts for materials and labor being awarded to out-of-state firms. Virginian newspaper contributors pointed out that "Chesterfield County has the finest granite and the mountains of Virginia have the finest timber in the world, but Government jobs go by favors."[42]

The first of three shipments of stone left Hallowell on May 6 and arrived at Yorktown on May 18; the first stone of the contract work was set on May 23. The second shipment arrived soon after, but the third was delayed and almost lost. A violent northeastern storm off Delaware Bay caused the three-masted schooner *A.H. Hurlburt*'s cargo of granite to shift. Fortunately, it was reported the wooden crates encasing the stone and allegorical figure kept it from any damage. However, the badly leaking *Hurlburt* spent several days lying at anchor off Cape May.[43]

The Cheney & Turnbull firm prepared Yorktown for the arrival of the stone, constructing a wharf to receive the cargo and a railroad to move it; it also provided derricks for handling the weighty blocks in addition to all the scaffolding used for construction. Once the ships arrived at the wharves, the boxed and numbered stone units of the monument were loaded onto the railroad and then drawn up the steep grade by a steel-cabled stationary engine.

Adjustments had to be made to the foundation, which had been laid in 1881 before the commission of artists had definitely defined the courses of stone. (Originally, it was six and a half feet deep, square, forty-one feet on side and bottom and thirty-one and a half feet on top.) Over the older concrete, fifteen inches of the same material was added to connect the level of the top with that of the bottom, finished with a facing of granite two feet wide.

The base courses of dressed blocks, six feet long by two feet thick, rose over ten feet by June 25. Richard M. Hunt specified the construction:

> *SETTING.—Lafarge cement to be used throughout. No cement to be used except on the day it is made. All stones to be floated in cement. Each course to be thoroughly bedded in mortar, and all vertical joints completely filled solid. Joints to be neatly struck that—no lewis holes to show. The stones composing the courses from and including the top course of the die to the base of the shaft of column to be clamped together with gun-metal clamps one inch thick, three inches broad and twelve inches long, with ends turned down three inches. The crowing figure to be bolted down by a gun-metal bolt 3 inches in diameter, extending 12 inches into bottom of the statue and running down 11 feet 6 inches through the top courses; 12 feet 6 inches total length. The three capping stones in pediments on each side of die to be secured by type metal dowels, run in a molten state, as may be directed.*[44]

Throughout construction, the stone that had been sunk to mark the height above mean low water was used as a reference point by the inspector, who examined and sighted the level of the first course for signs of foundation subsidence daily. Work continued through the July heat and humidity. The drum was set on the pedestal, and up went the three sections of the shaft, their joints hidden by ornamental laurel wreath bands. By the beginning of August, the monument had risen to forty feet and climbed higher with each addition. Local papers reported on the brief impressions of day tripping visitors to the site. Anticipation was growing for the completion date, set for October, and the next celebration of Yorktown's victory.

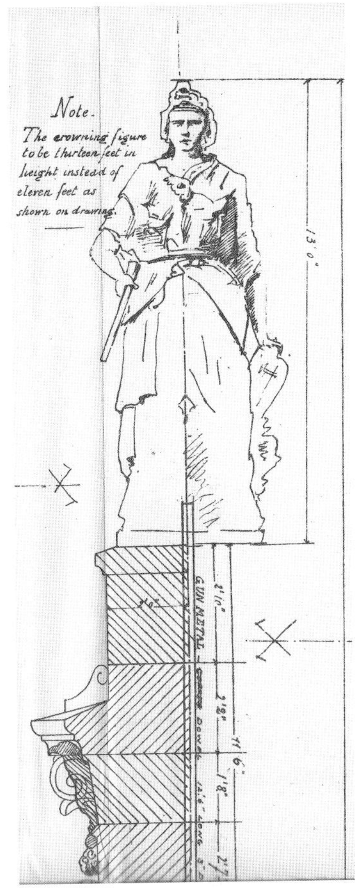

R.M. Hunt's architectural drawing, 1883. *Author's collection.*

During the work, only one injury was reported, that of William Carter of Boston, who fell thirty feet from the scaffold, broke his arm and was taken to Richmond for treatment on August 11.[45] A local young man, John S. DeNeufville, whose family descended from a French soldier in the 1781 battle who later settled in Yorktown, was hired as a replacement on the work crew. All hands were needed, as preparations were underway to raise the crowning figure to the top of the column the next day, August 12.

Unlike other Revolutionary War monuments being raised throughout the country since the centennials began, the Yorktown monument was not topped with a historic figure or soldier effigy. The capping statue for the monument was to be a classical female allegory like those that had come to embody the symbols of America, freedom and liberty. Before seeing the sculpture, many in the press referred to it as the "goddess of liberty," based on the descriptions and specs available to the public; the statue itself had no separate official title. The monument's official title as a whole was *The Monument to Alliance and Victory*. The symbols and emblems that sculptor

"Yorktown Monument, Alliance and Victory Monument." Rendering by R.M. Hunt, 1884. *Library of Congress.*

Ward chose were meant to convey those ideas. In the catalogues of works attributed to J.Q.A. Ward, the crowning sculpture is titled *Victory*. His early sketches refer to mythic figures like Athena, helmeted warrior goddess who carried a shield and spear, but by the time the final designs where approved, the figure had been softened to a more benevolent countenance of grace. It became a victorious figure carrying the nation's shield, with an outreached gesture offering the blessings of liberty.

Victory was a work of art in its own right, specified to be carved not of the Hallowell granite but stone from Westerly, Rhode Island, favored by the artist for its carving properties for statuary. J.Q.A. Ward was a famous and highly sought-after sculptor, producing one to three monolithic projects a year, especially through the centennial years. After the assassination of President Garfield in 1881, Ward was commissioned to sculpt a tribute to the martyred leader. It is therefore highly probable that *Victory* was not the product of a solitary artist chiseling away nonstop in his studio. Ward produced the plaster models of the figure and all the embellishments for the column and drum section. He then assigned them to the master stone carvers at Hallowell along with all the specs for the sculptures. These skilled craftsmen, mostly immigrants from Italy and Poland, would have roughed out the stone figure to near competition, and the artist himself finished the work, making corrections, adding the finer points and finessing the detail work of his vision. In this manner, Ward made several trips to Hallowell to supervise the carving of the caryatids and other embellishments by the stonemasons there. All of the monument's embellishments were to be carved out of the Rhode Island stone, based on the plaster of Paris models provided by Ward.

The figure known as *Victory*, *Liberty Herself* or *Goddess of Liberty* was raised to the top of the shaft on the evening of August 12 at about six o'clock in the presence of the secretary of war and other distinguished gentlemen.[46] The figure weighed eight and a half tons and stood thirteen feet, nine inches high and six feet, seven inches across from the fingers of the extended hands, making the monument in its entirety nearly one hundred feet above the ground. There had been some discussion among the contractors and commissioners in regard to which direction the statue should face. The first point being where to place the derrick and equipage for the raising, the other points were that of sentiment and symbolism. Should the figure face the actual site of the surrender of the British to the American and French forces, or toward the Moore House, where the Articles of Capitulation were negotiated? Perhaps toward the York River, where the French fleet was

Above: Close-up of the *Victory* figure, circa 1903. *Library of Congress.*

Opposite: Monument commemorating surrender of Cornwallis and the end of the Revolution, circa 1907. *Library of Congress.*

anchored, or the Chesapeake Bay, assuming that is where future visitors arriving by steamships would glimpse it first? It ultimately followed the artist's conception and faces out over the town and fields beyond.

The major installation finished and the scaffolding still in place, architect Hunt and sculptor Ward spent several days inspecting and then retouching the drum and figure. A twelve-foot-wide granite pavement was then installed to border the base to improve the appearance and prevent erosion. A careful yet brief consideration of installing exterior lightning rods on the structure was declined, deemed "unsightly" on such an ornate work. This fateful decision later played an important role in the monument's future.

In his closing reports dated September 25, 1884, to Secretary of War Robert T. Lincoln, Lieutenant Colonel of Engineers William P. Craighill looked toward the monument's future. In order to keep "meddlesome people at a distance," a fence would be installed around the twelve feet pavement. In a move to save money and create an appropriate visual effect, Craighill requested from the Ordnance Department condemned gun barrels and bayonets to be made into the protective fence, but this effort was not successful. A simple and traditional wooden fence was installed to be unobstructive to the view yet a deterrent to those who would seek to pass over it. Concern was also expressed about damage to the monument from "inconsiderate relic hunters" and the need to place a watchman on site constantly with a keeper's dwelling to be provided. The entire monument

Yorktown monument, circa 1903. *Library of Congress.*

project unexpectedly came in under budget by about $5,000, even with a $4,000 overage on the Hallowell bid due to unforeseen flawed stones. Craighill suggested these funds could be put forth to acquire a house for the watchman.

In October, all contracts for work expired. With the project completed in full, the beautiful new monument would be the glorious centerpiece of the 103rd anniversary of the Yorktown victory on October 19. While many who came to view the monument were filled with that soaring sense of patriotic

Column showing Yorktown shield. *Photo by Linda Williams.*

awe, others expressed their disappointment that nowhere among all the inscriptions on the commemorative monument to victory at Yorktown was the name Lafayette.

The finished product follows the standard Trajan's Column format, consisting of a shaft with a crowning figure, elaborated with a base composed of a podium in pediments and a sculpted drum in homage to contemporary French monuments.[47] As a war monument, it resembles many of the Northern "Soldier and Sailor" monuments that were commissioned at the end of the Civil War for city plazas and cemeteries. The interpretation of the column's design and symbolism was expressed in Ward, Van Brunt and Hunt's proposal:

> *Its characteristics of detail are also devised to give practical interest and significance to an architectural form which, without them would be to formal and cold for memorial uses. A column without decoration, but built in strict conformity with the consecrated conventions of proportion, is suited to sustain an entablature and play its part in the façade of a temple; but when conceived on a colossal scale and set up alone as a monument, it becomes meaningless and bald. When so used it is necessary for the architect not to content himself with making its proportions and details conform to*

the accepted formulas, and with justifying its existence by causing it to support a statue, but to lavish upon it all the thought and invention at his command with the object of making it a monument, of, as the Germans have it, "denk maal," a "think place."

In 1781, Congress put forth an act to erect a marble column at Yorktown, its chief purpose being to commemorate the surrender of the British and the alliance with France through emblems and a narrative of the event. It is unknown beyond that what Congress envisioned at the time. One hundred years later, it was deemed necessary to commemorate not only the event but also the outcome, requiring more than a column. R.M. Hunt's base had to accommodate all the narratives as well as support and complement the column. The monument is inscribed as follows:

South side:
AT YORK ON OCTOBER 19 1781 AFTER A SIEGE OF NINETEEN DAYS
BY 5500 AMERICAN AND 7000 FRENCH TROOPS OF THE LINE 3500 VIRGINIA MILITIA
UNDER COMMAND OF GENERAL THOMAS NELSON AND 36 FRENCH SHIPS OF WAR
EARL CORNWALLIS COMMANDER OF THE BRITISH FORCES AT YORK
AND GLOUCESTER SURRENDERED HIS ARMY 7251 OFFICERS AND MEN
840 SEAMEN 244 CANNON AND 24 STANDARDS
TO HIS EXCELLENCY GEORGE WASHINGTON
COMMANDER IN CHIEF OF THE COMBINED FORCES OF AMERICA AND FRANCE
TO HIS EXCELLENCY THE COMTE DE ROCHAMBEAU
COMMANDING THE AUXILIARY TROOPS OF HIS MOST CHRISTIAN MAJESTY IN AMERICA
AND TO HIS EXCELLENCY THE COMTE DE GRASSE
COMMANDING IN CHIEF THE NAVAL ARMY OF FRANCE IN CHESAPEAKE

East side:
THE TREATY CONCLUDED FEBRUARY 6 1778
BETWEEN THE UNITED STATES OF AMERICA AND

"Emblems of Alliance," south side. *Courtesy of Linda Williams.*

"Emblems of War," east side. *Courtesy of Linda Williams.*

LOUIS XVI KING OF FRANCE
DECLARES
THE ESSENTIAL AND DIRECT END OF THE PRESENT
DEFENSIVE ALLIANCE
IS TO MAINTAIN EFFECTUALLY
THE LIBERTY AND SOVEREIGNTY AND INDEPENDENCE
ABSOLUTE AND UNLIMITED OF THE SAID UNITED
STATES

North side:
ERECTED
IN PURSUANCE OF
A RESOLUTION OF CONGRESS ADOPTED OCTOBER 29
1781
AND AN ACT OF CONGRESS APPROVED JUNE 7 1880
TO COMMORATE THE VICTORY
BY WHICH
THE INDEPENDENCE OF THE UNITED STATES OF
AMERICA
WAS ACHIEVED AS WELL IN MATTERS OF
GOVERNMENT AS OF COMMERCE

West side:
THE PROVISIONAL ARTICLES OF PEACE CONCLUDED
NOVEMBER 30 1782
AND THE DEFINITIVE TREATY OF PEACE CONCLUDED
SEPTEMBER 3 1783
BETWEEN THE UNITED STATES OF AMERICA
AND GEORGE III KING OF GREAT BRITAIN AND IRELAND
DECLARE
HIS BRITANNIC MAJESTY ACKNOWLEDGES THE SAID
UNITED STATES
VIZ NEW HAMPSHIRE MASSACHUSETTS BAY RHODE
ISLAND AND
PROVIDENCE PLANTATIONS CONNECTICUT NEW YORK
NEW JERSEY PENNSYLVANIA DELAWARE MARYLAND
VIRGINIA NORTH CAROLINA
SOUTH CAROLINA AND GEORGIA TO BE FREE
SOVEREIGN AND INDEPENDENT STATES

Above: "Emblems of Peace," north side. *Courtesy of Linda Williams.*

Left: "Emblems of Nationality," west side. *Photo by Bill Coughlin, August 12, 2008, courtesy HMdb.org.*

Caryatids, thirteen maidens supporting the column, representing the first states. *Courtesy of Linda Williams.*

A Monumental Error?

J.Q.A. Ward's approved sketches and model of *Victory* depicted the figure holding a shield in her left hand and the right lowered and outreached with palm up. The completed statue has no shield and both arms raised in an awkward pose. As of this writing, no reason has been found for the change, and there are no sketches or written descriptions of the new pose prior to construction. Eyewitness John DeNeufville reported that in 1884, after the figure was raised, a sculptor had to finish the work "because the muscle of her arm was too big."

The official 1884 report of the monument's construction submitted by Lieutenant Colonel William P. Craighill to Secretary of War Robert T. Lincoln stated:

> *Architect Hunt and sculptor Ward…spent several days at Yorktown when the monument had been completed but the scaffolding not removed. A little retouching was there done to the crowning figure and drum in place.*
>
> *The drawings which accompanied my last annual report gave quite a full representation of the monument, and for that reason no details are given*

Sketch of Ward's crowning figure, 1883. *Author's collection.*

> *now. In a few particulars the monument as built does not conform to those drawings, but the differences relate to points which were subject to change in the specifications of the contract. The modifications were of an artistic character and were made by the commission who furnished the design.*

There is a clue here: it was uncharacteristic for the usually meticulous Craighill to not document the major changes made in the statue, either by description or illustration in his report to the secretary.

Another possible clue that there was something wrong with the statute's construction can be seen in magnification of R.M. Hunt's watercolor. He depicts the arms not as reaching out, but twisted and bent. The new pose made for much of the artistic criticism of *Victory* over the years; in their design with the new pose, Ward and Hunt did not take into account how the figure would be seen from the ground one hundred feet below. The figure was often described as startled or waving for attention. In the age before the telephoto lens or drone photography, no one was able appreciate the details of the lady.

It is the author's theory that a mishap befell the sculpture's pieces en route to Yorktown when the third schooner, carrying the sculpture, floundered off Cape May and the cargo shifted, perhaps damaging the shield that should have been held at the figure's left. The delay in that ship's arrival left no time to carve a replacement before the due date of the contract for the monument's erection. The artists also had other pressing installations to attend at the time. Being that the commission of artists (Ward and Hunt) answered only to themselves in matters of aesthetics, the quick and simple solution was to alter the position of the arms. Left in place without the prop of the shield, the figure's composition would have brought to mind the image of one begging alms, not offering liberty. It may have been easy enough to raise the left arm that would have held the shield to bring it into a natural palm-up position. Studying the right arm, however, there is an unnatural curve and an outfacing, bent cupped palm. It is easy to envision this was an arm originally in a lower position and turned to the right, as depicted in the sketches. With the arm turned over in an upraised position, the forearm had to be carved and contoured to attain a more anatomically correct appearance. This solution calls to mind the old saying "Good enough for government work."

11

SESQUICENTENNIAL

"Speculation and Preservation"

If a monument of architecture is like a "song without words," it certainly touches the mind and heart as much as it moves the senses.
—Henry Van Brunt

The monument completed, the celebrations over, Yorktown once again settled into its familiar routine. As the enthusiasm and interest of the centennial and the erection of the monument waned, all the grand plans and promise seemed to evaporate. The railroad coming near Yorktown remained in perpetual planning stages. No developers invested capital in the town. Yorktown continued to be a little riverside hamlet surrounded by farmlands, known to those visiting the area as a pleasant day trip to admire the new monument, picnic along the river shoreline and explore the surrounding mounds and trenches in the overgrown fields. In January 1885, the large centennial building at Temple Farm burned down. It was built and used during the anniversary celebration—and there were plans to develop a history museum for the proposed Lafayette Park—but the structure ended up being sold for a third of its cost and used for storing crops and harvest implements.[48]

The monument dominated the sparse landscape and amazed and delighted those who came to see it. Concern, however, was growing for the safety of such an important national treasure in such an isolated and unprotected area. Craighill had advocated for a watchman or custodian

Old colonial cottage, one of the most picturesque attractions of the sleepy old village of Yorktown, Virginia, circa 1907). *Library of Congress.*

to guard against relic hunters and "mischievous, inconsiderate persons." There was also a need to monitor the area for damage due to weather or other injuries that might occur. The Congress though, had appropriated only $100,000 to build the monument, with no provisions for its future maintenance and upkeep. There was a temporary watchman to act as keeper and custodian until 1886. "The old weather beaten soldier, Saul, watched it [the monument] as closely and takes as much pride in it as if it were his wife."[49] Private Peter Saul had to quarter in the old shed erected in 1881 as a construction office, described as "a shanty, and unfit for human habitation, necessary to raise an umbrella indoors when it rains."[50]

Craighill suggested the $5,000 surplus from the monument fund be used for upkeep, but there was no follow-through. Advocates for the monument like the Maryland Historical Society lobbied for such protection, and travel writers of the day commented on the need. In Yorktown, Kate Nelson, great-granddaughter of the famed Thomas, offered the old Nelson House for sale to the government for the $5,000, an idea that drew much local support. She later offered to lower the price to $2,500 for the sake of government preservation of the house. Over several legislative sessions, Congressman Libby of Virginia put forth bills to appropriate funds to purchase the Nelson House to be used as a keeper's residence, but they neither survived the process nor were approved by Congress.

Keeping up appearances being paramount to the social and cultural elite of the day, frustration grew among those who worked to present the South's culture as on par and as modern as the North. Unlike the historical societies, which found the monument's location sacred and appropriate, the cultural arts patrons and clubs found Yorktown to be an utter embarrassment, just as they had during the centennial. Those in the social strata of Virginia's

The Nelson House and Main Street, Yorktown, Virginia, circa 1902. *Library of Congress.*

cities felt wholly ashamed and blushed to bring visitors to Yorktown. Worldly travelers who expected a groomed park-like memorial, similar to the European models, or even the garden cemetery park style overlooking a quaint historical seaside resort encountered the wonderful, inspiring monument languishing in a wasteland of scrub and mud. Critics described the area as peopled by a "larger than comfortable" number of poor Black farmers and a few "dull, uncultured Whites."

A movement began to form, advocating for moving the monument to a more suitable location, such as Richmond or Norfolk, somewhere it would be seen by more of the population and could be presented in a more fashionable surround. Organizations petitioned on behalf of their locales to receive the monument; however, what these city and cultural organizations overlooked was that unlike many other monuments raised during the memorial frenzy following the end of the Civil War, *The Monument to Alliance and Victory* was a congressional authorization stipulated to be raised at Yorktown, funded by the United States as a whole, not a local citizens' concern. This was a national monument on federal property and would not be moved. The chorus of discontent raged on, and the drumbeat to raise funds to move the monument continued. However, once the independent cost estimates for moving and re-erecting such a structure came in at a total far above the $100,000 cost to build the monument, the drum stopped beating. Though the harsh critiques continued, their volume faded into acceptance. "Sentiment and historical propriety both demand that the Yorktown monument shall be at Yorktown, whether it is viewed by few or many."[51]

In 1892, the custody of the monument was by order of the secretary of war transferred to the quartermaster general of the army, to be considered as part of the Yorktown National Cemetery. A new picket fence was installed around the one-acre plot surrounding the monument and the grounds put in good condition.[52]

Another criticism of the monument's location came from the historical purists, who felt that rather than in the town, the monument should have been placed at the actual site of the British surrender. Lossing's 1859 book mentioned this sentiment voiced by the men who could still confidently identify the exact spot. The site of the surrender negotiations, the Moore House, was also thought to be an appropriate location for a monument, though the house was beginning to take on a monumental status of its own. But the monument was a fait accompli, it was where it was, yet there was among the history-minded the desire to have some acknowledgement of

Old Yorktown, Virginia, and monument commemorating Cornwallis' surrender, circa 1907. *Library of Congress.*

not just the area, but the very piece of ground on which the momentous event took place. One such person was John W. Shaw. In 1895, Shaw was a Union Civil War veteran and serving as the superintendent of the National Cemetery at Yorktown. Shaw was aware that the location of the once marked spot was in the vicinity of the cemetery and that a previous obelisk had existed where Nelson's Poplar trees originally stood. Shaw investigated the surrounding area and found what he believed to be the stumps of those long-gone trees. Here on a dirt road, behind the Black residents' graveyard boarding the Union Cemetery, Shaw decided to erect a marker so the spot could be memorialized.

Monument commemorating the surrender at Yorktown, the Shaw Monument circa 1900. *USN 900195 National Archives.*

As the government was not convinced about the accuracy of the location, Shaw found no support to install any form of marker or monument at his chosen site. Further academic research would have to be engaged before the government would ever commit to such a project. Passionate in his project, Shaw decided to build a monument using his own funds and labor. Shaw collected granite pieces from the riverfront and bricks from the site of the county courthouse destroyed in 1863 to assemble his structure. It would be a twenty-one-and-a-half-foot-tall obelisk constructed of the brick, covered in cement stucco, sitting on a six-foot-square base of granite, ornamented with cannon balls and a painted wooden plaque. This structure, too, had its admirers and detractors among the visitors to Yorktown. The little monument became a popular tourist must-see, and in the new age of photography, it became a postcard picture to represent the historic place.

After Shaw's death in 1907, no one kept up the monument, and it had become an overgrown crumbling derelict in danger of collapsing by 1920, a curious site for anyone who happened upon it. In 1934, as the National

The Shaw Monument remnants at NPS maintenance yard, circa 2013. *COLO-NPS Photo.*

Park Service was coalescing around its interpretation of the battlefield at Yorktown, a study was done on the "Shaw Monument." Park superintendent Floyd Flickinger wrote: "From our recent studies we have every reason to believe that this gentleman with his good intention was in error as to the exact location."

The Park Service dismantled the monument and carried it to a wooded area nearby, literally exiling it to the backwoods of history. The monument, now in pieces, stayed in this location, off the developed tour road, where glimpses of it could be seen by the observant in the fall of the year when the foliage thinned. In 2005, about one hundred yards from where Shaw's obelisk stood, with funds from the Society of the Cincinnati heritage group, a wayside marker was installed at the place determined to be the true surrender spot. In 2013, the Park Service moved the sections of Shaw's obelisk to its maintenance yard and later donated pieces of it to the Yorktown Historical Museum.

At the dawn of the twentieth century, Shaw's Monument was not alone in neglect. Funds were not procured to provide a residence for a monument keeper. Such duties as would have been assigned to a keeper now fell under the supervision of the cemetery superintendent, William Van Dree. While Yorktown began to be advocated as a tourist locale to the ever-increasing leisure traveler, the monument, its star centerpiece, came under criticism. The granite continued to whiten and glisten if not sparkle in the sunlight, yet the surrounding grounds horrified and offended many. Citizens demanded a more respectful frame for this work of art and heaped criticism on the national government for allowing such a condition to exist.

> *No care at all is taken of the honored pile: the fence surrounding it, rotten and broken down, allows the cattle to graze on its sacred ground: its*

> *symmetrical lines and substantial base covered with a fungus growth, elicit nothing but an unstinted amount of denunciation by those who visit it.*[53]

> *A rank growth of weeds disputes possession of the sacred soil with the remains of a rotten fence and general dilapidation prevails.*[54]

> *The memories of our fallen heroes cry out at this neglect of the stately statuary which marks the spot near which they covered themselves with glory.*[55]

Criticism, public outcry and a need to save face eventually prompted the government to visit the monument and perform maintenance. In advance of the impending 1907 Jamestown Exposition, Secretary of War William Howard Taft arrived on the Island of Jamestown accompanied by representatives of the Association for the Preservation of Virginia Antiquities (APVA), the Army Corps of Engineers and local congressmen to select a site to erect a National Tercentennial Monument to coincide with the exposition to be held in Norfolk. Leaving Jamestown, Taft and his advisors visited the College of William and Mary and then continued on to Yorktown, where his yacht *Dolphin* was at anchor to serve as his accommodations. Before departing the area, the secretary of war toured and assessed the cemetery and monument site at Yorktown, which would also be a destination for visitors during the exposition. Taft was most likely greeted by weeds and free-range livestock. Advertisements were immediately sent out, and a few months prior to the May 1907 opening of the exposition, contractors arrived to work on the monument site. The grounds were groomed, walkways improved and a new iron fence installed around the site.[56]

The Jamestown Exposition was, by an act of Congress,

> *to provide for celebrating the birth of the American nation, the first permanent settlement of English-speaking people on the Western Hemisphere, by the holding of an international naval, marine, and military celebration in the vicinity of Jamestown.*[57]

The APVA had started the campaign in 1900 to formally celebrate the three hundredth anniversary and promote the preservation of their holdings on Jamestown Island. The idea was supported by many groups and politicians, especially President Theodore Roosevelt, an avid student of American history, who signed a $3 million appropriation to create the exposition. The powers that be, however, deemed the small, swampy, undeveloped isle of

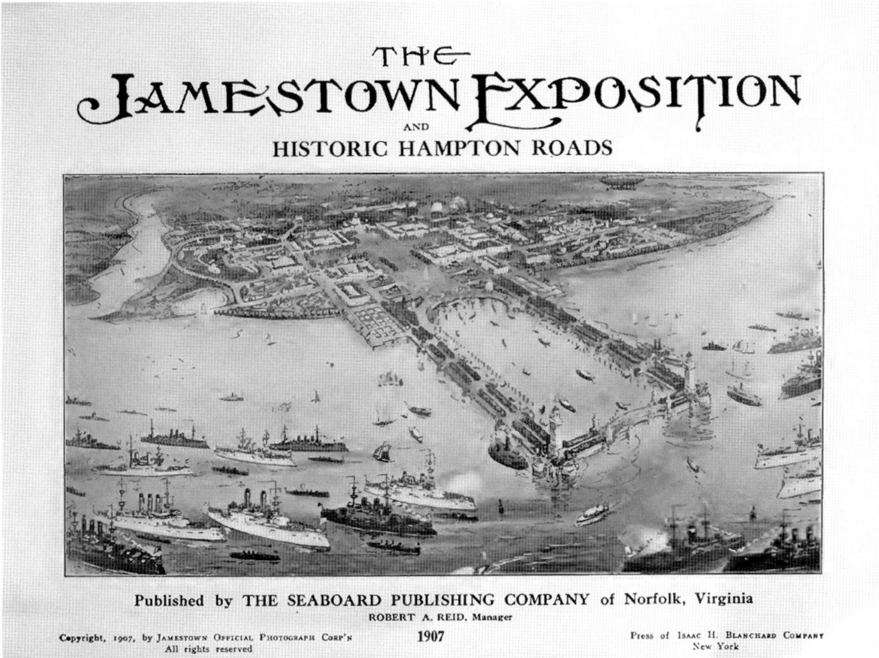

Event program for the Jamestown Exposition of 1907. *Internet Archive, Getty Research Institute.*

Jamestown unfit for such an envisioned event. The city of Richmond was the first considered site, but the planning committees chose Sewell's Point, a piece of land equally accessible from the centers of population, Norfolk, Portsmouth, Hampton and Newport News. The choice eventually benefited Norfolk's aspiration to be the seat of military command. Sewell's Point had a position on the James River that would also be more accommodating to the participation of the military. In a short time, this rural site underwent a modern transformation with the installation of infrastructure that would put it on par with any small, self-contained city. Ten years after the closing of the exposition, the unused site was taken over by the government during World War I, and the ready infrastructure and site development helped speed the development of Naval Station Norfolk, the world's largest naval base.[58]

The exposition was a six-month affair opening April 26 through the closing on November 1. It was on the scale of a world's fair with a purely American theme, and all the states and territories of the union sponsored pavilions and exhibits of their resources and histories. A showcase of the modern marvels of the day, electrically illuminated pavilions and midways exhibited the latest creations of industry, the discoveries of science and the initiatives of government. Foreign and domestic cultural pavilions showcased the history of Virginia Indians, the progress of southern African Americans and the culture of the honored guests from Japan. Entertainments and amusements abounded, such as Wild West shows, river tours and band concerts. The main theme of the event paled in comparison to what would become the "coming-out party" for President Roosevelt's new navy, the "Great White Fleet." Dignitaries and ministers from around the world were invited to witness the modern American armada on parade in the harbors of Hampton Roads. After the exposition, these modern ships, all painted white, were sent around the world, proclaiming America's future dominance of the world's seas.

Jamestown Island itself saw only one grand public day, May 13; the exposition hosted water carnivals and boat races while the APVA held exercises to "most appropriately celebrate the three hundredth anniversary of the settlement."[59] Virginia governor Claude A. Swanson and British ambassador James Bryce attended to provide the appropriate oratory and dignity for the occasion. Visitors arrived by steamboat to swarm over the island, view the sacred remains of the church tower and other visible ruins, listen to the various orations of the dignitaries and picnic along the shore. The APVA worked to present the island site in its best light, with the installation of the Colonial Dames' gift of a bronze gate, the construction of a memorial church and other recently donated plaques and memorial markers.

To mark this great event in American history, the government also authorized a monument. This tribute to the country's beginning was appropriately placed at the site of Jamestown. Congress appropriated $50,000 for the marker, and Secretary of War Taft was charged with selecting the grounds on which to erect it. In June 1906, land was acquired from the owners of Jamestown Island, a tract of 450 feet by 125 feet, running down to 175 feet at the riverfront.[60] That same month, James Knox Taylor, supervising architect of the treasury, completed the plans for an exact miniature of the Washington Monument to be 100 feet tall on a base 100 feet square composed of granite. Requests for bids to build the shaft were sent to contractors, and by October, there were only two bidders: Harrison Granite Company of Maine and the Norcross Brothers Company of New Hampshire. Both bidders were in excess of the $50,000 appropriation, causing architect Taylor to review and reduce the specifications for ornamentation and approach in hopes one of the firms would take the job for the $50,000.[61] The monument was

Jamestown Tercentennial Monument postcard, circa 1920. *Author's collection.*

constructed of granite from the Mascoma quarry in New Hampshire, a light buff-gray stone speckled with black and even grained.[62] Credit may be due to the Norcross Brothers, pioneers in the new method of "general contracting," which raised the monument by April 1907. Though it was completed in time for the exposition, there was no formal unveiling or dedication ceremony.

Another monument planned for Jamestown's anniversary was a tribute to Pocahontas, memorializing the vital aid she and her people provided the struggling settlers. The Pocahontas Memorial Association engaged the sculptor William Ordway Partridge to create a statue of the Indian princess.

The model was completed in time for the exposition, yet funds were lacking for a bronze cast. A plaster replica was displayed at the exposition in Norfolk. Fundraising by subscriptions from various societies—Daughters of the American Revolution, Colonial Dames, APVA and others—fell short of the goal of $10,000. In December 1912, the U.S. Senate passed a bill to appropriate $5,000 toward the monument. The statue was cast, and a dedication ceremony was held in June 1922. The sculptor composed a figure more resembling the Plains Indians rather than the Algonquin Virginians, adding to misunderstanding and myths. Originally, the statue stood eighteen feet tall with its pedestal, which over the years was removed and the statue situated in various places due to the recent ongoing archaeological digs. She now stands at ground level; her arms and hands are a shiny coppery bronze from years of park visitors affectionately holding them.

The new century was bringing with it a more mobile generation of citizens. Steamship excursions brought more of the public to Yorktown in search of diversion. Religious, social, military and political organizations all found the area a pleasant gathering place to picnic, socialize and politic. With growing exposure to the area, as during the centennial, came the desire to preserve the historic grounds. Ancestry groups like Daughters and Sons of the Revolution and Colonial Dames of Virginia began to advocate and lobby for the government purchasing the five-hundred-acre Temple Farm and turning Yorktown into a National Park.[63] Joining that property with its Moore House, the cemetery and the monument, would ensure all were properly cared for. With each October observance, whether called "Surrender Day," "Thomas Nelson Day" or "Yorktown Day," interest in developing the area was growing. Even more appealing, after twenty years of rumors and promises of a railroad coming through the area with an electric cable car service, the plan of grading and paving roads was now gaining steam.

Yorktown started to draw the kind of attention it had always craved—*investors*. Retired midwestern businessmen out of Chicago and Cincinnati started to buy up open land and depressed properties like the Nelson House to refurbish as summer homes while they bought stock and joined the boards of emerging Virginia companies and utilities. To these men and others, Yorktown was ripe for business ventures. Referred to often as the Chicago capitalist syndicate,[64] men like Captain George P. Blow and Judge Howard Ferris spearheaded much of the land speculation and industrial development.

All of the future planned ventures relied heavily on the elusive and perpetual negotiations with the Chesapeake & Ohio railroad to reinstall the six-mile spur from its station at Lee Hall to a terminus at Yorktown,

Pocahontas Monument postcard, circa 1925. *Author's collection.*

a track that had been laid to serve during the centennial and removed immediately thereafter. In fact, since 1850 Yorktown residents had tried to convince the railroad to come to the area with no success—the road saw no profit in farmers and oystermen. Now, however, it displayed a mild interest in the proposed ventures it could contribute to and profit from. Among these were:

- A small steamship line based in the York River, to free the port from its dependence on the Baltimore lines, could bring goods to the larger markets of Norfolk, Hampton and Newport News;
- tour excursions three times a week bringing in visitors to spend a few hours in Yorktown;

Main Street of quaint old Yorktown, circa 1907. *Library of Congress.*

- a shipbuilding dock, to bring in local craftsman to construct workboats and pleasure yachts;
- the Jamestown Cement factory, built 250 yards from the monument site, to take advantage of the natural marl and shell resources along the riverbanks;
- investments in infrastructure, such as a $40,000 pier to service the factory and the grading and paving of roads;
- a coal yard and distribution terminal;
- an ice plant and cold storage warehouse for the seafood industry.

These and other ventures were planned, hyped or started during the early 1900s, only to fall apart owing to various impediments, the major one being the railroad. One thing after another impeded negotiations: stalling on the railroad's side and missteps on the investor's account. In their zeal to encourage development and profit, the Yorktown trustees granted the Cement Company all the deep-water rights to the waterfront for ninety-nine years, which ended any possibility of a rail line–owned steam ship development there. The railroad had also insisted that the investors procure the land rights of way for all proposed roads and rail routes, which they failed to do even though in years prior landowners had offered their rights for free to the railroad. Without the support and commitment of the railroad, bonds and funding fell through on most deals. Projects under construction sputtered to a halt or never get any further than the planning and promotional advertising. The first twenty-five years of the 1900s kept the County Clerk's Office open full time as deeds, and properties constantly changed hands and corporations formed and reformed to chase the next big idea. By 1913, Yorktown was so lethargic a place that the president of the United States of America, a Virginia native, Woodrow Wilson, could dock his yacht at the wharf and leisurely stroll about the town visiting the Nelson House and the Moore House and not be recognized.[65] But it was still attractive to investors. Then, with the advent of the automobile, driving clubs formed. Day trips to Yorktown by these groups would inspire advocation for the investment into improving the roads.[66]

The alarming pace and prospect of development renewed the call from historic preservation groups to lobby government officials to purchase the lands around the monument to create a National Park, but no move was made to acquire Temple Farm or any other historic building. The military, however, by presidential proclamation, was acquiring eleven thousand acres of surrounding farms as well as forcibly removing the entire community of Black farmers and oystermen known as Charles' Corner. Situated upriver from Yorktown, these lands were to be used for weapons storage and firing ranges. In the same area, the Dupont Company was building an entire new factory town of ten thousand workers seemingly overnight to support the manufacturing of dynamite.[67] The navy brought scores of visiting sailors to Yorktown, as its ships used the York River for shakedown cruises and maneuvers in anticipation of America joining the war overseas.

During the late 1910s and the entry into World War I, the Virginia Peninsula and its ports, like Yorktown, became strategic to the military. New naval installations were developed on the York River. Land below

USS *Langley* (CV-1), the first aircraft carrier at anchor in the York River, circa 1922. *NH 63545 U.S. Naval History and Heritage Command Photograph.*

Temple Farm was purchased by the navy for a fuel depot, and above Yorktown the old colonial plantations of Bellfield and Ringfield became airfields and munition depots. The War Department insisted that the surrounding counties improve their roads between Newport News and Richmond to facilitate the impending needs of the war effort.[68] The York River, with its deep channel, again was an asset to a naval power and began to see the same type of attention that had brought it fame in the 1700s. Yorktown, with its new naval investments, and the port of Norfolk were pitted against each other for the development of a new naval base and headquarters for the Atlantic fleet. The largest argument, however, against Yorktown would once again be the lack of proper roads and the absence of a railway presence, all of which Norfolk had.[69] Yorktown would not be the naval base but serve with support facilities. Even the soaring one-hundred-foot monument would have to cede its air superiority as the navy began to develop aircraft carriers, using the York River for test flights before and after the war.

After the War to End All Wars was over, optimism ushered in a new prosperity for America. In Yorktown, the monument was the centerpiece of the speculative 1920s. A new cement road was completed from the rail station at Lee Hall to Yorktown—now all the town streets right up to the monument were paved—to the delight of the auto clubs. The auto traveling public offered the access to Yorktown that many hoped the railroad would bring. Visitors could now travel by train to Lee Hall and then hire a car or take a bus to Yorktown.

> *The concrete road which has just been completed will make it a veritable "Mecca" for pilgrims who want to worship at the shrine of American Independence.*[70]

To support the increased tourism, the Yorktown-Virginia Corporation leased seven acres adjacent to the monument from the government to create a park to accommodate the hundreds of tourists who would arrive on Sundays.[71] Investors once again saw great opportunity in Yorktown as a leisure destination, and plans to build a grand hotel in the area were now put forth. The optimistic atmosphere of the 1920s would see various competing groups arise with plans for Yorktown's future. These groups would often be symbiotic in their goals yet come to different ends.

THE DAUGHTERS OF THE AMERICAN REVOLUTION. From the beginning of the century, the national DAR had continually lobbied local, state and federal officials to acquire and preserve the landscape of the battlefields in Yorktown as a National Park and to protect the historic buildings still standing. Finding support but no results from legislators, the ladies worked with the majority landholders like Captain Blow and Judge Ferris on agreements to fence off and detour encroachment on the historic earthworks and landmarks in the fields. In 1922, Emma Leake Chenoweth formed the Comte de Grasse Chapter of Yorktown, which then set a goal to acquire and preserve the Old Customs House, and commissioned the investigations of historic data for various plots targeted for development. By the mid-1920s, the national chapter's campaign was gaining more support in Congress, and the Yorktown chapter became more involved in preservation and promotional and fundraising efforts. The ladies would also be one of the leading forces developing plans for the impending sesquicentennial of 1931.

THE YORKTOWN HISTORICAL SOCIETY. Formed in 1909 by local and national citizens, members also included the Descendants of Declaration Signers group led by the great-grandson of Tench Tilghman. They held their meetings in the Nelson House until it was purchased by Captain

The Proposed Yorktown Country Club & Manor Hotel, from the prospective membership material, circa 1924. *NPS Reference Resource.*

George P. Blow, who also became a member. The goals of the society were to protect and restore the remaining colonial-era buildings and battlefields; publish and promote books, pamphlets and photographs; and contribute to the curriculum of schoolchildren.[72] This group lent its knowledge and assets to other groups trying to drum up commercial interest in Yorktown, serving as guest speakers and tour guides for both academic endeavors and orientation meetings with prospective investors.

THE YORKTOWN HOTEL CORPORATION. Formed by those early speculators still looking to invest in Yorktown and headed by Judge Howard Ferris, the majority landholder in the area. The corporation sought to create a resort to rival the favored destinations (Pinehurst and White Sulphur Springs) of the growing sports-minded, wealthy leisure class. The vision was the grand $2 million Manor Hotel and Country Club, built with the most modern and scientific construction. Housing three hundred rooms, it offered every entertainment and luxury: a casino, a spa, indoor saltwater pools, opulent ballrooms and world-class dining. Surrounded by formal gardens and a premier golf course that incorporated and preserved the features of the battlefield, tennis courts, bathhouses, a yacht haven, fishing excursions, foxhunts, hunting grounds for small game and fowl, the lands around Yorktown offered infinite sporting opportunities.

THE YORKTOWN WORLD FORUM. At the end of World War I, an international peace movement arose, centered on the academic institutions. These groups set out to work for global peace among nations, through the diplomatic arts, open exchanges and forums for negotiations. In 1925, the College of William and Mary established the James Monroe Chair of International

Relations, to be part of the Wythe-Marshall-Monroe School of Government and Citizenship there to be affiliated with the Yorktown World Forum. One of its goals was to restore and maintain the battlefields as a shrine to liberty. The grounds would house the forum in facilities that would equal Geneva, Versailles or The Hague. An auditorium that would seat fifteen thousand was planned, grouped with historic buildings, libraries and residences for world diplomats.

> *The forum will be located on the surrender ground—an area sacred in the political history of mankind. The buildings will take the form of a great classical temple, with affiliated units interpreting in symbol the eras of history and the epochs in the history of democracy in the world featuring the republics of ancient and medieval times.*[73]

"The Yorktown Movement," as it would be called, hoped to foster greater relations with world powers and counter the emerging tenets of socialism and fascism. Proponents saw their venture as a place where diplomats, world leaders and those who influenced them could meet and mingle and be converted to the "American Religion of Liberty." The Duke of York, future King George VI of England, accepted the honorary presidency of the forum as well as membership in the County Club, though he would never get to visit and participate. The forum's plans paired well with those of the Hotel Corporation, and they shared board members and investors, Judge Ferris being the major facilities developer.

THE WAR DEPARTMENT. As war production wound down and the pandemic of Spanish flu closed the Dupont Penniman dynamite facilities after 1918, the navy increased its landholdings by taking over that vacated facility. Legislation was introduced in 1920 to establish a military park at Yorktown, but hearings would not take place until 1924. The secretary of war appointed a civilian committee to investigate and report on the feasibility of creating a park around the known fortifications and those recently exposed by the preliminary clearings made by workmen for the Hotel Company. Conflict arose between the department and the Hotel Company, since their designs on the battlefield overlapped and the company plans were in progress. Judge Ferris and his company had no objections to the government's plans as long as they did not disrupt operations. However, the congressional bills put forth to develop a military park took an "all or nothing" approach, to include authorizing the condemning of the entire village and depriving the State of Virginia of jurisdiction over any roads crossing the park.[74] This plan would come under criticism by the local congressman Otis Bland, who strongly advocated for a park at Yorktown but sought to protect the local interests. The War Department began to doubt the proposal of need for a National Park since most of the landmarks and part of the 1,147 acres the government deemed necessary to create such a park were already incorporated into the hotel grounds. Golf engineer William S. Flynn built the course that was then in use to protect the "war relic zones." But after all the years of lobbying and legislating, the government was now on course to establish a park, and where there is a will and government money, there is a way.

THE RESIDENTS OF THE TOWN. While the residents of Yorktown and most residents of the peninsula supported the establishment of a National Park on the idle lands around Yorktown, the great fear was that it would entail condemning and confiscating homes and homesteads. There was opposition to the government inclusion of any buildings and businesses in the town within the park. Among the older residents of the area, only decades past the Civil War, was the ingrained distrust of a federal government that would impose its will on an unwilling populace. There was a great fear among the White residents of Yorktown that they would be treated no better than the Black inhabitants of Charles' Corner. Complaints and concerns were also raised against the construction of the

Mines laid by the U.S. Navy in the North Sea, stored in open fields near Yorktown, circa 1920. *NH 123960 Naval History and Heritage Command Photograph.*

Navy Mine Depot by nearby landowners, fearing the worst outcome of their stockpiles of munition stores.

Preservation of the battlefield was the common goal of all groups that focused on Yorktown, whether their goals were commercial or philanthropic. The grand Manor Hotel laid a cornerstone and erected a concrete and steel frame in 1926. The next year, the officers of the Hotel Corporation were embroiled in a legal battle against the government. The navy planned to make the weapon's base at Yorktown the East Coast dump site for all the leftover war munitions. The idea of impending danger only yards from recreating guests had generated bad publicity for the area. By 1928, after supply and labor delays, bond deals and funding had begun to fall apart—as did the finances of many investors. The World Peace Forum movement and its donors faded away after America declined to join the League of Nations. The bills were now coming due all over the country for the rampant grandiose speculation of the 1920s. The only enlightenment that could be obtained on the battlefield of Yorktown would be an improved golf swing.

The year 1930 dawned with a much-changed atmosphere in Yorktown. The Yorktown Historical Society had disbanded and reorganized as the Yorktown chapter of the Association for the Preservation of Virginia Antiquities or the APVA. Throughout the 1930s, this group, along with the Works Progress Administration (WPA), focused on the preservation and transcription of historic documents in the files of York County. They also acquired as a gift from Judge Ferris in 1928 the foundations site of Secretary Nelson's house in order to save it from a planned road construction.[75] Later, the APVA sponsored an archaeological study and preservation project and erected a memorial tablet. At last, President Hoover signed the "Cramton Bill," creating Colonial National Monument, to include Jamestown Island, lands for the Colonial Parkway and the Yorktown Battlefield, for the preservation of the historical grounds and structures there, including the monument. Yorktown was now the concern of the National Park Service, which then began a geological survey of the entire area.[76]

Emblem of the National Park Service. *NPS History Resource Guide.*

Judge Ferris passed away in December 1930, leaving the steel frame of his failed hotel venture standing on a bluff over the river, a monument to what could have been.

The 1940 Colonial National Historical Park brochure. *U.S. Government Printing Office.*

Golf balls still flew over the battlefield for a few more years but not as they had during the tournaments of the '20s. The final company that Judge Ferris had organized was the Jamestown Corporation, chartered to take over and hold his properties until the government could make an appropriation for its proposed Colonial National Monument Park. Ferris received $200,000 and interest for all his holdings, which included forty-three separate parcels of land, encompassing nearly 2,500 acres outside of Yorktown. These were York River Cliffs, Edge Hill Farm, French Quarters (Beer Farm), Palmatory (Surrender Field), Terrapin Point, Pigeon Quarter and Waterview Farm. Lots within the town's limits included the Old Yorktown Hotel and Swan Tavern site, along with all the land of the undeveloped second golf course. With no grand tourist facilities, no political science temple, no more opportunity for industry and the gathering dread of an economic depression taking hold, Yorktown was back to where it started, full of awe and disappointment. Standing watch, high above it all, was the *Victory* monument and the lady with her gesture of calm as the next wave was about to crash on the fields of Yorktown: the 1931 sesquicentennial.

As the 150th anniversary of Tench Tilghman making his ride to Philadelphia approached, once again the nation would turn its attention to Yorktown. Five decades since the centennial of 1881 and Yorktown was in no better shape to handle the onslaught of visitors that would descend upon it. It had only two small hotels and a few cafés, still a provincial village. The Ladies of the DAR worked for many years prior to prepare for the celebrations, but this was more than the state and local society groups could manage on their own. This was to be a national spectacle that incorporated all the resources and financial appropriations of government, the military and its logistics, the politicians with their connections and state, city and county governments and their contributions.

Months before the celebration, Yorktown was once again invaded by several armies. First came the National Park Service. The new National Monument superintendent, staff and assistants oversaw the clearing of the battlefield and preparing it for the celebration activities, issuing specifications for construction work and awarding contracts for work on the grounds. Under the command of Brigadier General Stanley D. Embick, commanding officer of Fort Monroe, hundreds of soldiers set up a self-sustained tent city encampment and began preparing the grounds, building roads, footpaths and docks; constructing infrastructure to provide water and electricity; erecting exhibition tents; and designating latrines and parking spaces. The Marines prepared to assist in traffic control and enforcement along the newly constructed roads the State of Virginia had installed to Yorktown.

The 1931 October observance of the victory at Yorktown was an exposition or small world's fair–type production with a colonial and Revolutionary theme. There were pageants, pavilions and exhibits sponsored by states and history groups. Large attraction included a colonial fair, a harvest festival and an Indian village exhibited by the people of Pocahontas, the Mattaponi and Pamunkey tribes. Numerus demonstrations, plays and reenactments of period life, along with a showcase of the Virginia Department of Agriculture and its products featuring a zoological exhibit of the state's indigenous animals. There were large dance pavilions and band stands for concerts and, of course, concessionaires of all sorts inside huge restaurant and refreshment tents.

Historical military unit encampments from various states joined in the military exercises, parades and reviews. The navy assembled an impressive fleet of its most modern war vessels. The battleship on which President Hoover arrived was greeted by a twenty-one-gun salute fired by twenty-eight ships. The most modern cruisers escorted the French delegation to Yorktown when they and their ships arrived as they had 150 years before

Yorktown Sesquicentennial Expedition, October 20, 1931. *NH 109618 U.S. Naval History and Heritage Command Photograph.*

in the Chesapeake Bay. By day, the army and navy's lighter-than-air ships hung in the sky above the parade grounds. At night, planes from Langley Field flew down the river, illuminated by searchlights while being fired on by antiaircraft guns shooting blank rounds. The planes dispersed a hail of red flares into the night sky to simulate hits, thrilling the crowds below.

National, state and civic cooperating volunteer organizations from the Boy Scouts to the Red Cross all performed services under the direction of the army during the four-day spectacle. Wave after wave of people crashed into the fields of Yorktown, Some 10,000 soldiers and sailors plus various military bands paraded in review before the president; over 3,000 people were involved in the pageants and exhibits. The National Park Service had a complement of 57 temporary rangers on hand, and there were uncounted vendors, contractors and volunteers to assist the public. The estimate for the final day alone was 150,000 attendees. People arrived by trains and steamships as well as buses and cars. A partial count of vehicles in the lots maintained by the army numbered 97,000. Yorktown and other nearby cities hosted world leaders and descendants of historic persons. National

View of the government memorial in Yorktown, Virginia. Behind it is a U.S. Army airship, circa 1931. *Sueddeutsche Zeitung Photo/Almay Stock.*

and state officials all came to pay tribute and memorialize the birthplace of independence and liberty.

Temporary victory arches and pylons were erected along roads and on the celebration grounds that paid tribute to the original states. Roadways and trails throughout the grounds were lined with interpretive signs and markers. The history and descendant organizations practically paved the town in bronze tablets of commemorations to the lives of heroes and the heroic dead.

Standing in the midst of it all, glowing in the illumination of the newly installed spotlights each evening, was *The Monument to Alliance and Victory*.

Just as quickly as the crowds rushed in, they receded. Grandstands and temporary infrastructure remained on the fields for another year until they were dismantled and taken to another event. It was all in the hands of the National Park Service now. They were on hand during the celebration to introduce the public to parks in distant parts of the country like Yellowstone through their exhibits of artifacts, photos and models. They also presented future plans for the surrounding area and generally promoted the conservation

Monument illuminated by newly installed spotlights, 1931. *Proceedings of the United States Yorktown Sesquicentennial Commission. Library of Congress.*

of America's wonders. It was their task to morph the celebration grounds and improvements into a park setting that would interpret the story of the battle and preserve the site for future Americans to enjoy. By Executive Order 6166 on June 10, 1933, the War Department transferred the jurisdiction of the National Cemetery and the Victory Monument to the Interior Department for inclusion in the Colonial National Monument Park under the management of the National Park Service. There were grand plans for the park to be the ultimate outdoor museum and shrine of the American story from its colonial beginnings to its Revolutionary climax, just as soon as all the details, such as the rapidly declining economy, could be worked out. Even before the celebration of 1931, funds for park development were being delayed. Roadwork on the parkway to connect Yorktown to Williamsburg was put on hold along with other larger infrastructure projects. The treasury deficit prompted the government to cut back on all expenditures as the country slid deeper into the Great Depression.

The Virginia Peninsula's agrarian economy was slightly cushioned by the military presence in the region. Yorktown was still a favorite picnic spot for locals and servicemen alike, and golf was still played on the course by those who could afford it. The Park Service amended and altered its plans based on available funding and staff. Larger projects were put on hold, and more attention was put toward research and archaeology surveys. Park projects resumed after the election of Franklin D. Roosevelt and the implementation of New Deal works programs like the Civilian Conservation Corps, putting men to work on public projects to modernize and benefit the nation. Building National Parks was one such benefit. Camps arose in the Yorktown area, hiring men to do the manual labor of building the park's infrastructure; four camps set up in the area known as "Camp Victory" were units consisting of Black men. These men participated in archaeology surveys as well as artifact preservation, building the roads, demolishing buildings and reconstructing earthworks on the battlefield. Their workshops turned out all the handcrafted items needed for historic building restorations and artillery reproductions. They managed forestry and landscaping, installed utilities and built protective seawalls for the waterfront. Ironically, the CCC rebuilt all the fortifications and trenches that residents long ago had sought to erase from the landscape.

The men of the CCC were instrumental in the summer of 1933, when a powerful hurricane struck the area. Record flooding and damage to communities and infrastructure were devastating. The Victory Monument weathered the storm well, exceeding the 1883 wind pressure survey

Men of the CCC reconstructing fortifications on the Yorktown Battlefield, circa 1935. *NPS Photo.*

conducted by the Corps of Engineers during construction.[77] Atop the spire, *Victory* reached out and gestured calm as the men of the CCC arrived with equipment and labor to help clear out all the debris and dead livestock and assist with the stabilization of structures in the rural riverfront farms and villages. The work of the CCC continued on through the Great Depression. In 1936, the Park Service acquired the golf course and the property on which the hulking frame of the failed Manor Hotel stood. The following year, the workmen set charges of TNT at its base structure and brought it down in sections, removing rubble in between blast days. The steel was sent off for scrap while the cement and brick debris was used in the seawall construction on the waterfront below.[78]

The late 1930s once again saw the specter of war on the horizon. There was more and more activity at the navy installations near Yorktown. The CCC camps began to thin out as men, equipment and funds were diverted to other projects. The war overseas threatened to come ever closer. The Red Cross drummed up relief efforts for Europe, American trade and shipping became threatened and the veil of neutrality was wearing thin. Then on the infamous day in December 1941, as the Pacific fleet burned and sank at Pearl Harbor, the war machine of this country roared to life as patriots once again went off to battle. The Victory Monument watched over all the

USS *Yorktown* (CV-5), 1937. *NH 50333 U.S. Naval History and Heritage Command Photograph.*

activities of the homefront, its calm stance firm against the fear of U-boats in the York River, the blackouts, the air raid drills and the increased security around the military bases. The Victory Monument stood as a reminder that liberty and freedom were worth fighting for. What had been won in 1781 would not be lost today.

In June 1942, during the Pacific battle of Midway, Yorktown's namesake aircraft carrier (CV-5) USS *Yorktown* was torpedoed and later sunk. A month later, as the clouds of war hung over America, storm clouds also descended on the village of Yorktown. During an electrical storm on the night of Thursday, July 29, 1942, after fifty-eight unprotected years, the one-hundred-foot-tall monument, the tallest object for miles around, standing on a high bluff overlooking a river, was struck by lightning.[79] The strike blasted off the outstretched arms and decapitated the figure of *Victory*. The falling head struck the figure's hanging veil and feet before crashing into the base steps, landing on the ground and scattering pieces of granite in its wake. Across the back of the figure was a large crack, and a white streak ran down the shaft into the thirteen dancing figures of

Above: Damage to monument's base from head impact, July 1942. *NPS Photo.*

Right: *Victory*'s lightning severed head, July 1942. *NPS Photo.*

Monument after lightning damage, July 1942. *NPS Photo.*

What a bolt from the blue (or black, since it was late Wednesday night when the storm occurred) can do in a millionth of a second to man's handiwork is exhibited here. The fragments broken by a lightning—stroke from the top of the statue on the Victory monument are seen here—the head practically whole, the arms shattered. (Daily Press Staff Photo).

Broken fragments from the top of the Victory Monument, August 2, 1942. *Daily Press Archive Photo/TCA.*

the drum. It was feared the shock had loosened the monument, making it unstable. Two mighty symbols of America's first war victory destroyed within a month. There was too much ominous symbolism to contemplate, but for Yorktown, it was again familiar territory.

After the grounds were cleaned up, secured and the investigations and reports made, the monument was left as is. There were no resources available to even consider repairing a monument from one war while fighting another. Yet what was left of *Victory* atop the column stood tall and, though maimed, was still beautiful, a work of art, Yorktown's own version of Venus de Milo. All who came to gaze on her could not help but be filled with soaring awe and pitiful disappointment.

Part III

Septaquintaquinquecentennial

"Art and Artifacts"

During the 1930s, Yorktown was in constant motion; the sesquicentennial's aftermath and its changes to the landscape ushered in the next phase of development in Yorktown, creating the long sought-after National Park. This was uncharted territory for the National Park Service, which had in its care since 1916 the jurisdiction of vast, sparsely inhabited wilderness. At Yorktown it had the charge of not only preserving but also restoring a landscape—a landscape that would have to weave around military bases, private holdings and a village that was the continuous seat of governance for the County of York. State, county and village authorities along with all the various historic and preservation groups all had their own vision of what the park would be. Park superintendent Floyd Flickenger had to exercise all his diplomatic skills as the service began to build on the park's master plan, which had to redirect with every cut in funding allocation as the economy sank ever deeper into the Depression. With a limited staff to start, the NPS focused on gathering the research and selecting the areas of the most historical interest to guide future projects. The Roosevelt administration's work programs brought the influx of men and equipment with the CCC that would advance the infrastructure plans of the park, tearing down the post–Civil War buildings and failed speculation projects, then reconstructing and restoring the buildings in the colonial village footprint. Revolutionary War field defenses were being reconstructed in tandem with archaeology assessments. "It is almost impossible to dig anywhere in Yorktown without striking traces of Colonial culture."[80]

The 1955 Colonial National Historical Park Brochure. *U.S. Government Printing Office.*

The Moore House also underwent a complete restoration, returning to its 1781 appearance. Planned construction of the road that would connect Yorktown with Williamsburg and then Jamestown was surveyed while rights and permits were pursued.

Each October, observers gathered around the Victory Monument for the usual orations, pageants and military parades. Every year offered something new for attendees to tour as the park progressed. Further plans and development of the park came to a halt with the outbreak of World War II. The construction of the parkway ended at Williamsburg, and the CCC camps disbanded as men were called to war or redirected to the war effort. Plans for the park were further modified and efforts focused on the archaeology at Jamestown and academic research. The October anniversary celebrations were held by small representatives of local groups or canceled altogether during the war years.[81] The most excitement Yorktown saw in these years was in November 1943 when a warehouse at the Navy Mine Depot exploded. The effects of the blast were felt as far as thirty miles away in Norfolk. Though the town was the closest in proximity to the base, no historic buildings or the monument were affected; however, some businesses on the waterfront were damaged by the concussion.[82]

Rumbling of another kind was heard in Yorktown, as the Park Service began to receive complaints about the closure of the golf course. While the park's master plan called for eliminating the course immediately, for the sake of goodwill it had remained in operation while the NPS finalized acquisition from the owners and during the surveys and archaeology studies conducted on the fields. The course's benefit as a tourist draw was also evaluated and considered during that time. The advent of the war and its climate of rations and scarcity provided the means to end its existence and to proceed with the reconstruction of the fields,[83] erasing the last imprint of those big dreams of the 1910s and '20s for the area.

World War II's end brought a new battle to Yorktown, that for the future of the monument. During the war years, patience was a virtue—no one expected the government to divert precious men and materials to repair the monument when so much was needed for the war effort. By 1947, however, America was seeing a rise in peacetime prosperity and a return to domestic concerns. It was now time to do something about the damaged monument to victory, not only for its own sake but also for the psyche of the populace for whom the monument had become its civic identity. Sixteen-term congressional representative from the First District of Virginia Schuyler Otis Bland led this new charge. Since 1918, Representative Bland had championed the efforts

Park ranger inspects erosion of Redoubt No. 9, September 1953. *NPS Photo.*

of the DAR to create a park at Yorktown, initiating much of the preservation legislation over the years while also encouraging any financial development he thought beneficial to the district, like the long-debated bridge crossing of the York River at Yorktown. Bland kept the monument's condition at the forefront of the Interior Department's attention with frequent letters and inquiries. The department's slow response prompted Bland to state:

> *I hope the repair of the monument will not take as long (100 years) as it did to construct it.*

Assistant Secretary of the Interior Girard Davidson's response created a divided debate among those concerned:

> *It is quite possible that repairs to the storm damaged allegorical figure of Liberty are not feasible. An entirely new figure may need to be sculpted. Despite our efforts to secure interest in the project from several contractors none has admitted interest or ability to handle it. The National Park Service is endeavoring to determine as accurately as possible what the cost and arrangements must be to cover such a special and major repair. The monument is of granite which apparently was quarried at Hallowell Maine, and by the Hallowell Granite Co. there in 1883. If we are fortunate enough to trace down a plaster model of the original figure we will be able to form a more accurate estimate and can likely reduce the cost of the work to be done. But, the National Park Service now has no appropriation to cover such a project.*[84]

For the next two years, through editorial comments, petitions, orations, resolutions and letters to congressmen, a public debate raged between three factions:

THE CYNICS. These balked at the $50,000–$100,000 estimated cost of repairing or replacing the monument. Pointing out that "other famous statuary figures, like the headless Winged Victory of Samothrace, and the armless Venus de Milo did not lose their symbolism, and were even revered for the tribute exacted by time and the elements. Until the cost of granite arms and heads goes down, it looks as though Yorktown's Victory must join this distinguished company of amputees."[85] Best to tear it down completely and install something more modest and cost-effective. These commenters also mocked the emerging marketed reputation of the area as the "Cradle of the Nation" and Representative Bland as its "gallant representative."

THE ESTHETICALLY MINDED. To those who appreciated the monument as a complete work of art, the course the Park Service was pursuing, that of simply replacing the head and arms of the statue, would not do. A monument to victory was taking on a new meaning to a country that had just won a world war, and a patch job would be an insult to those it commemorated and those who so recently gave their all for its enshrined ideals—"Make It Real Art." This group advocated for a completely new statue to be commissioned and executed not by a stone contractor but by a true professional artist. Remove the remnants of the original, give it a place of honor on display and install a new, similar figure, making it a whole work once again

THE LOCALS. For seven years, the monument had stood as is, and those in the area had become accustomed to its new appearance. There was an affection for the original sculpture that a generation had grown up with and a "leave things be" sentiment that saw the damage as part of the story. Other civic and social members of the community advocated for the restoration in some form as soon as possible. Suggestions deluged congressmen about what should be done about the monument, ranging from doing nothing to reconstructing a monument on the scale of the Jefferson and Lincoln Memorials. The residents of Yorktown felt that being the ones who had to live day to day with the site, they should have some say in the matter. The ladies of the DAR offered to head a campaign to raise any funds and support any work that the government could not appropriate, while Representative Bland did his upmost to keep pressure on the Department of Interior.

Military personnel in the area also had a true affection for the monument. The sight of *Victory* up high and dry on the bluff was a relief to many returning sailors. In the USO at Yorktown, a young seamen confided to the townspeople his gratitude to be back in the little town again and like *Victory* he was going to stay on dry ground. In 1945, army colonel Robert N. Mackin, serving with British Intelligence in Cairo, wrote to his wife:

> *I've travelled all around this place. I've visited the Pyramids, I've seen the Sphynx and the Nile, but all I really want to see is a headless statue on the York.*[86]

At the beginning of 1949, the prospects for having the monument repaired were postponed indefinitely by the Park Service. A letter to Representative Bland stated the NPS's authorization for physical improvements in 1950 had been cut from $10 million to $3 million, but it would consider the inclusion

Representative Schuyler Otis Bland, circa 1921. *Library of Congress.*

again for the 1951 funding.[87] But the government moves in mysterious ways. On Wednesday, July 12, the Senate Appropriations Committee approved $65,000 for a repair fund that was not part of the Interior Department appropriation bill.[88]

Six months later, the monument's gallant champion, the Honorable Schuyler Otis Bland, congressional representative of Virginia's First District from 1918 to 1950, passed away.

With funding now secured, the search commenced for an artist to take on the task of sculpting a new figure for the monument. In October 1949, it was announced that a contract had been awarded and plans were now underway for the erection of a new statue to replace the damaged figure. And for the next seven years, the double-edged sword of awe and disappointment hung over Yorktown.

The artist selected for the Yorktown contract was the renowned Oskar J.W. Hansen, a Norwegian-born naturalized citizen. A creature of self-promotion, Hansen had a larger-than-life—and somewhat unverifiable—biography before he took up sculpting as his profession. He started out as a cabin boy with the merchant seamen of Norway, circling the globe five times, later to join the French Foreign Legion in North Africa and studying sculpture with the great Auguste Rodin in France, before immigrating to America by jumping ship and swimming ashore. Hansen then served in the American army. A man of many and varied pursuits, Hansen dabbled in prose and poetry, astronomy and physics, architecture, history and botany—his credentials may have been dubious, but there was no doubting his ability as an artist and his influential body of work. Hansen was no stranger to government projects. He was commissioned in the 1930s for a sculpture installation at the "Boulder Dam" Project (later renamed Hoover Dam). His sculptures, tablets, plaques and inlaid star charted floors were the apex of public art installations of the New Deal era and became icons of the Art Deco style.

Hansen was most likely chosen for the project based on his years of association with government officials during the dam project; he had cultivated many contacts and friends among the congressmen, senators and legions of bureaucrats. Hansen understood that for artists during the Great Depression, the government works programs would be their only hope for commissions and a wellspring of funding. Hansen made his home and studio not far from Washington, D.C., in Charlottesville, Virginia, at an estate on Pantops Mountain, part of Thomas Jefferson's original land holdings. Privy to early knowledge of the project, he quickly submitted a plaster bust as a model to replace *Victory*'s head for consideration. The fifty-seven-year-old artist's style was still very much in vogue and sought after. His Art Deco style had entered the '50s space age, and his decorative pieces morphed into what would be called "mid-century modern," increasing his relevance and feeding his voracious ego. For all the eccentricities, self-aggrandizing and smugness that can come from true talent, it could be said that Hansen was a true genius. The National Park Service was to discover that Oskar Hansen was a man of awesome artistic reputation but a public relations disappointment.

The $65,000 appropriation signed by President Truman and contract awarded to Hansen allocated $59,000 for the sculpture and the balance to be used for the installation of lightning protection and repairing any other miscellaneous damage. The contract called for an identical statue to be completed within two and a half years on April 11, 1952. By December 1949, Hansen had submitted a plaster model of a reproduction of the original sculpture, which was approved by the Park Service.[89] This was the beginning of a stormy and costly relationship that spanned two decades.

Opposite: *Winged Figures of the Republic* sculpture at Hoover Dam by Oskar Hansen. *Photo, Carol M. Highsmith, Library of Congress.*

1950

Hansen conferred with the Park Service and requested a search for the original designs and specs of the 1884 work. The sculptor later claimed that such information was not provided to him until four weeks after he signed the contract. Specs of the monument were part of the War Department reports for 1884, but it is unknown if investigations were made into the records of Hunt, Ward or Van Brunt, the original artist committee.

On his frequent visits to Yorktown, Hansen made the rounds of the local social groups, introducing himself and making his presence and task known to residents of the village as well as local members of the press, carousing and glad-handing as good as any politician.

Visits were made to the North Carolina Granite Corporation in Mount Airy, North Carolina, where Hansen selected two granite blocks equaling 34,489 pounds to be delivered to his mountaintop estate in October. There he built a studio around the "mountain of stone" to be used in the work. He now had eighteen months to deliver his commission.

Granite blocks in the quarry of the North Carolina Granite Corporation. *Courtesy of the Mount Airy Museum of Regional History Photograph Collection.*

1951

During this year, Hansen set out to sculpt his version of what he titled *Liberty*, using a pneumatic carbide chisel on the blocks of granite. *Liberty* was carved in two sections: the head to torso and then the torso to feet.

Hansen made various visits to Yorktown, conducting studies and surveys of the monument. During his visits, whether before a member of the press, a politician or just a passerby, Hansen expressed his opinion and assessment of the monument's artistic relevance and style. In the years since its installation, the work had had its fair share of artistic critique, positive and negative. Hansen, however, took his distaste for the standing column to the level of personal vendetta. The snobbery of his elitist artistic persona ignited a several-years-long feud with his patron, the National Park Service. Hansen constantly expressed his opinion that the Victorian style of the 1884 monument was out of place as a monument to a colonial area. He personally preferred a simpler design, "pre-Hellenic rather than neo-Classic." Hansen found no inspiration in the column's symbols or narratives and began to put forth his desire to replace the column entirely.

Another October observance carried on beneath the shattered monument. Onlookers gazed upward at the strange sight of a swarm of bees hovering above the shoulders of *Victory*, where honeybees had constructed a hive.[90] "Sweet Freedom" was the constant remark of the day.

Hansen had only a few months left to deliver his replacement statue. He wrote letters to the Park Service, the secretary of the interior and his other Washington contacts regarding his opinion that the shaft might have to be replaced.

1952

In March, with only one month until the statue's contracted due date of April 11, the work was nowhere near ready for installation. Hansen received a reprieve due to a national shortage of copper needed for the lightning protection.

The completion of the project was delayed pending the government's ban on the use of critical materials for nondefense projects by the Park Service, and Hansen was given an indefinite extension.[91]

While there was much disappointment to all concerned that there would be no new sculpture this year, Hansen avoided scrutiny; the monument's plight was overshadowed by the completion of the long-awaited bridge crossing the York River.

May saw the opening of the George P. Coleman Bridge with as much or more fanfare than any of the October observances; ships filled the river, and dignitaries lined the shores. The Coleman Bridge was a modern marvel and cost $9 million. It spanned 3,750 feet, connecting Yorktown to Gloucester Point at the narrowest part of the river, making it the largest swing span bridge in the country. The bridge would have a great effect on not only the area but also the state as a whole. Rural goods could get to different markets, and travel north to south would also enhance the business development of the peninsula, making U.S. Route 17 the shortest highway route from Hampton Roads to Washington, D.C. Everything the residents of the past had hoped the railroad would bring was now possible with the automobile and the bridge.

The Park Service was less than enthusiastic. From its inception in 1916, it had to walk a fine line when it came to its overall mission of protection and preservation. Without public support for that mission, the NPS could never succeed, and the only way to gain pubic support was for the public to have access to these protected wonders in order to gain an appreciation. Twenty years before, the Park Service defeated a bridge project by a private corporation, and over the years, the competing interests of the state, navy and Park Service had clashed. The Park Service, along with area history groups, decried spoiling the pristine vista of the colonial era, horrified at the thought of a monstrosity of cement and steel standing as an anachronism against the park and upstaging the monument. The DAR also protested the bridge crossing location and advocated that it be moved farther upriver. But the needs and resources of the state won out, the bridge footprint being on the established state ferry dock and the river under state jurisdiction. The NPS attendance at the dedication was limited to reserved smiles and handshakes, much to the amusement of local residents, who saw the event as the Park Service getting a taste of its own medicine after years of government confiscation of private lands to build the park.

By October, the new bridge had become part of the scenery and would provide easy access for visitors to enter the park as the annual observance got underway. Attention once again turned to the monument, and questions about the passing of ten years since the fateful lightning strike bedeviled the Park Service.

In his interactions with officials and admirers, Hansen casually criticized the style of the monument. Now he turned the subject from his uncompleted sculpture to the soundness of the monument itself, casting doubt on the stability of the column and making his concerns known to all his congressional contacts. He made this accusation as the Park Service began to request a due date for his work.

Superintendent Edward A. Hummel left this situation to his assistant George F. Emery, as he took a new position as head of the park in the Great Smoky Mountains. It was a larger yet less stressful situation for Hummel.[92] Hansen and his public theatrics were now Emery's problem and soon that of a new superintendent.

1953

Hansen escalated his campaign against the monument's column, writing letters to anyone and everyone in Washington, D.C., he thought would aid his cause. He used every encounter with the press to push his theory about the shaft's soundness and ability to support his new work. To the press, he admitted that the figure he had been working on for four years was only three-fourths complete, but it was larger and would weigh more than the original figure. He made frequent personal inspections of the site and conferred with the park's new superintendent, Stanley W. Abbott, who pressed Hansen in March for plans to install his sculpture and fulfil his contract's new due date of October 11. Hansen's visits to Washington, letters and lobbying efforts brought unwanted critical attention to the park, as the NPS began to receive inquiries from officials in government about the monument's stability.

Hansen presented various theories about the column that struck safety concerns within the Department of the Interior, prompting an inspection by a special crew of the National Capitol Parks in April. A scaffolding was raised around the monument to determine the exact damage done by the lightning bolt in 1942. The crew then investigated Hansen's various claims that the granite crumbled to the touch, was possibly hollow or if it was solid, requiring more expense to install the lightning protection required.[93]

Dr. D.W. Kessler, former chief of the building stone section of the Bureau of Standards, stated that the monument was structurally sound but should be protected from lightning and reinforced with a steel shaft at the center to counter high-velocity winds. Otherwise, the general feeling was that the

Yorktown Monument "should last a few thousand years." Another inspection was needed to determine if the column was hollow, which would allow the park to install the lightning deterrent by the time Hansen delivered the new statue on October 11.[94]

Hansen, meanwhile, still questioning the usability of the existing granite stone, continued his protests against the column, saying, "The monument should be taken down, re-designed and rebuilt…[and] made in keeping with the simplicity of the Revolutionary War era." Hansen suggested to Superintendent Abbott that the $4,500 allotment for drilling a hole for a lightning arrestor and miscellaneous repairs should instead be given to him to design a scale model for a new shaft. After receiving no reply, Hansen wrote to Secretary of the Interior Douglas McKay in July, arguing for changing his contract to "obtain a sanely constructed and adequate monument." Assistant Secretary Orme Lewis then met with Hansen and stated he would be glad to consider a new shaft if Hansen could provide $300,000 from private sources, the estimated cost of such a project.

In September, Hansen was granted another six-month extension to his contract while the park investigated the possibility of a hollow in the column and a method of installing a lightning apparatus.

By November, Hansen's critical campaign against the monument had begun to turn loud and personal. To the press, he stated that rather than see his figure placed on the column, "which is unsafe and also very ugly," he would be willing to refund the government its money given him thus far. It would be "perpetrating a hoax on the American people on their most important battlefield…to preserve a monument so badly designed and constructed that it became a failure against the forces of nature after only fifty-eight years." Citing his letter to Secretary McKay:

> *I wish to make plain…that one who like myself follows seriously the profession of sculpture can render unto Caesar only the things that are Caesar's. For the great God-given gift of being an artist, we make answer for our integrity only to the Great White Throne.*
>
> *To ask me to perpetrate, on the battlefield at Yorktown, a composition in sculpture bastardized according to the collective idea of a government bureaucracy, is asking of me, not only the services of my body, but the devastating perdition of my soul. If any of my work goes to Yorktown, it will stand there backed by a reputation I have worked hard to acquire. The compromising of that reputation is beyond the power of any government on earth to demand.*

Hansen told the press that if no agreement could be reached with the government, he would buy back his figure and

> *would consider seriously giving it (when completed) to Syngman Rhee, President of the Republic of Korea....I believe that in years to come he may stand as champion like Patrick Henry and Thomas Jefferson of the ideals of democracy and freedom.*

Continuing to air his grievances in public, Hansen stated that thus far the government had paid him $20,567.29, of which $5,567.29 was the cost of the stone from the quarry. He claimed that due to his expenses, the contract had cost him $100,000 in lost work, travel and providing an "equalized" climate for the stone to protect it from splitting. To offset his debt, he had to sell part of his mountain property for $50,000 to keep going and was now in debt.[95]

Superintendent Abbott pressed to respond to Hansen's statements, replied:

> *I am sure from Mr. Hansen's point of view, he is right, since a sculptor has natural interest in the design of the shaft, which will carry his work. However, the present shaft was placed here in 1881 and was designed by a commission in New York, composed of prominent architects or designers who designed a piece currently in vogue in the day.*
>
> *Our engineers have been reasonably convinced that the shaft is stable. At the present time, the National Park Service has no money to undertake the design and construction of a new shaft.*
>
> *No doubt some people will be in sympathy with Mr. Hansen's opinion, he being an artist in his field. I would not venture a guess as to how many people will feel otherwise. However, many may feel the present shaft is itself historical and has artistic merits.*[96]

Both sides of the debate divided community groups; even the ladies of the DAR seemed split on the subject. The regents of some chapters expressed agreement with and support of Hansen's option for change, while other chapters preferred the more historic preservation of the column. With another Jamestown anniversary approaching in 1957, this time to be within the park at Jamestown, the head of the 350th Anniversary Commission expressed that one way or another the hope was for the monument to be whole by the time of the event. All groups concerned—especially the people of Yorktown—were anxious for the work to be done and expressed surprise in the added expense of the project and the reason for all the delays. Most agreed that it would not be wise to install a new figure if the shaft was unsound and a more thorough inspection might be needed, yet no one could understand why Hansen had taken the commission in the first place if he did not want his work placed on the existing shaft based on his "artistic integrity." Few understood Hansen's argument—if the monument had been built in 1781, it would be worth saving, but being built 100 years later in the taste and fashion of those times, it was inappropriate and disposable, yet the figure he was carving 175 years later, in *his* own taste and fashion, was appropriate. The editorial comments of the day began to question Hansen's motive to replace the entire monument as less than artistic and more financial.

In early December, Hansen wrote to request a meeting with President Eisenhower's assistant Sherman Adams, emphasizing his concerns for public safety around the monument and a lack of response from Superintendent Abbott regarding replacing the shaft. He would not get his meeting but received a letter from the Park Service officially rejecting his request to replace the shaft, citing the structural reports and the service's desire to not alter the design of the monument as constructed in 1884.

Once again, Hansen promoted his case to the press, with less attention to artistic sensibilities. He put himself forth as a champion of safety, challenging the Park Service assessment. Noting the early discovery of a metal rod that served to anchor the original figure into the shaft, Hansen asserted, "Some part of the thunderbolt, which extends perhaps a foot into the old figure will have to be removed or I will not be able to attach the present figure." To remove this impediment, he would have to "knock a hole in the present shaft, which is already insecure," or remove sections of stone from around the rod. Either, he declared, would be "extremely hazardous." The new *Liberty* figure was not made to fit the rod because he did not know it was there.

"No one will be willing to write insurance" for persons to work on the shaft "or to bring equipment under it." "The shaft should be brought down with dynamite."[97]

Hansen requested in a letter sent through department channels to the secretary of the interior for "verbatim, certified copies of the reports" declaring the monument safe, "including the official signatures of each of the board partaking in the inquiry which declared the present column safe: together with engineer's drawings showing eccentricities now existing in the column.…This information is absolutely necessary for reference in applying for Workmen's Compensation Insurance and Performance Bond."

> *I refuse to be physically or morally responsible with the Park Service, for setting the scene into what might certainly become a sort of Mayan or Aztec blood sacrifice of American labor.*[98]

On December 27, the NPS announced that Hansen's appeal in his fight to have the shaft replaced was turned down and that the service saw no reason why Hansen should not deliver the figure and carry out other terms of the work by April 1954. While in Washington, again, still trying to meet with Secretary McKay to argue for a column worthy of his figure, Hansen's cringeworthy comment on hearing the announcement raised the ire of many area residents:

The importance of *his* figure, he said, "represents Liberty, not Pocahontas or little Wampum."[99]

This prompted editorial commentators to exclaim, "Read your contract," and draw conclusions that Hansen's main concerns were not safety or esthetics but personal profit and ego and that more time should be spent in the studio rather than in Washington. Once again, at the end of the year, Hansen had four months left to deliver his statue. The New Year, however, saw the beginning of a new battle at Yorktown.

1954

In January, Hansen was determined to go over the heads of the Park Service and meet directly with the secretary of the interior. During the meeting, he again put forth his opinion on the shaft's soundness and proposed a new design of his own. He envisioned his figure on a shaft that would be flanked by flag poles on either side that are taller than the work itself; a properly grounded shaft and the flag poles would be a sure lightning deterrent. The conference ended without a decision in Hansen's favor. Secretary McKay's statement was that Assistant Secretary Lewis, who had jurisdiction over the parks, had made the decision and a reversal would be up to him after any consultations. Lewis stated it was doubtful the decision would change.

By February, Hansen's constant protests and visits to D.C. had gained the attention of Chairman Ben F. Jensen (R-Iowa) of the House Interior Subcommittee on Appropriations. Representative Jensen and members of his committee planned a visit to Yorktown to gain firsthand information on the area and assess the shaft, stating:

> *I think this great monument of freedom should be improved. I felt someone had to take the lead because in the past 20 years it appears the previous administrations did not pay too much attention to it.*[100]

In April, Jensen put forth a $50,000 fund toward relocating the existing monument to Surrender Field and a start toward building a new shaft and other improvements. Hansen's contract was extended another year to come due April 1955. Chairman Jensen also planned his visit to the area later in the month. This news found no welcome in Yorktown as it circulated through the residents, who did not care for the idea of the monument being moved outside of the town. They did not quite believe all the insults being hurled at the column by "outsiders" and disliked all the suggestions being made by Hansen and Jensen. The only man deemed qualified to comment on the construction of the old monument, John S. DeNeufville, stepped forward into the public debate. He was a young man, all of fifteen in 1884, when he joined the construction crew after a worker was injured. At eighty-four, DeNeufville was the only person alive who had seen the inner and outer construction of the shaft. He detailed how the concrete foundation laid in 1881 sank ten feet underground and was allowed to settle for four years before the first block was placed.

> *Move the Victory Monument? Its shaft is unsafe? The whole thing's going to fall down in 25 years? Crazy....*
>
> *Of course it's a solid shaft. I know, because I saw every block put in place....Fall over, Push it over, Move it around, I think not....*
>
> *People don't understand how solid and heavy that monument is.*[101]

When Chairman Jensen and his group arrived in Williamsburg on April 20, most of the time was taken up reviewing plans with committees for the upcoming Jamestown 350th event and touring those locales. Jensen said his visit to Yorktown on the twenty-first would be to "look, listen, and learn." What he learned was that the Park Service insisted that the monument was sound and Hansen's figure should be placed atop it as contracted. He heard from the residents their disbelief that their tax dollars would be used to move a perfectly sound monument from its place in history, and he looked at the monument for himself. Early in the day, National Park Service director Conrad L. Wirth and Superintendent Abbott presented all the engineering data for the chairman. Hansen later met the visiting group at the monument to present his observations in his usual dramatic tone of panic. The sculptor said that the only thing holding the monument together was the figure on top, and if it were removed the whole thing would fall—he refused to go up there again. It was later observed that Hansen and Director Wirth engaged in an argument aside from the group. Chairman Jensen was of the opinion that the old monument should be worked on, but a new one near redoubts 9 and 10 or Surrender Field could also be built to feature Hansen's work. Jensen came to the following conclusions:

> *I looked at Hansen's figure and it is a wonderful piece of work. I am only interested in placing it where it should be. It should be where the folks would like to have it and in a place worthy of the figure.*
>
> *I came here to try to work out a solution only after others (Virginia Senators) had refused to have any part in the matter. I suggested a solution—now it is up to the people to decide what they want.*
>
> *If the (Senate) decide against the $50,000 appropriation who are we (Representatives) to tell them how to spend money? It isn't often that I recommend such an expenditure, but I feel this one is worthy.*[102]

At the end of April, while a $50,000 appropriation was approved within the Interior Department appropriation bill for the next year to permit the Park Service to design a new shaft, questions were raised by the Senate Interior Appropriations Subcommittee Chairman Cordon (R-Oregon). During a hearing on the Park Service budget, Senator Cordon received a letter from the DAR offering a suggestion that if his present work was not compatible, the sculptor should design a new figure that would be in keeping with the style of the present shaft, and he agreed. When Director Wirth explained Hansen's objection to his figure being placed on the existing shaft, Senator Knowland (R-California) remarked:

> *It is a tendency in this country to get rid of anything old, while most other countries in the world treasure historic spots.... The sculptor was employed to design a figure, I don't know that it is his decision as to the shaft.*

Senator Knowland said he would consider it "most unwise" to appropriate $50,000 for a new shaft that would ultimately cost $150,000 to $300,000.[103]

Later in May, Hansen addressed the Senate Interior Appropriations Committee to plead his case for a new shaft. This time, he added a new twist to his argument, stating that he had been "told" by Dr. Edward Riley, former district historian at Yorktown, that the monument was erected over a cemetery. He claimed soldiers of the Civil War Peninsular Campaign were buried there (a misconception to this day based on early 1900s letters describing burials at the National Cemetery as "close to the Surrender Monument," meaning the Shaw Monument). Another accusation of sacrilege that Hansen brought forth was that the Park Service planned to build a parking lot around the monument. (Plans for the development of Yorktown by the Park Service show large parking areas situated some distance away but none in the vicinity of the site.) In his customary dramatic style, Hansen declared:

> *Where the dead were not permitted to conclude their eternal rest, there must be the macadam of a parking lot.*[104]

Back at Yorktown, Superintendent Abbott had to issue a statement to the swarming press:

> *As far as is known here, no authority exists for the belief that the area ever was used for a burying ground.*

Though Hansen remarked many times that he would give the government back its money rather than see his figure placed on the old shaft, Abbott pointed out to the press that Hansen had made no formal request or attempt to do so. The attention to these events in the press riled the residents of Yorktown once again who firmly did not want two separate monuments in Yorktown. Editorial comments advised Hansen to "keep his chisel going and his mouth shut."

As a result of the congressional hearings, the House allotted $50,000 to make plans for a new monument in a new location. The Senate, questioning the need, omitted it from the Interior Department Budget. In committee, a compromise of $15,000 was appropriated, limited solely to study and rehabilitate the old shaft.

In December, scaffolding once again surrounded the monument as Charles Whitney and his staff of the New York engineering firm of Ammann & Whitney climbed and surveyed every inch of the shaft, tapping with specialized tools, using magnifying glasses and taking notes and photographs. Whitney withheld any judgment until he and his staff analyzed his findings along with both external evidences, internal computations and the study of original construction reports. The results were not available for several weeks.[105]

Scaffolding installation around monument base, September 1956. *NPS Photo.*

Hansen remarked on the inspection and coming reports:

> [The engineer, Charles S. Whitney,] *made a fine impression on me and I believe he will make every effort to give a sound engineering verdict. However, whether that verdict will be acceptable from an esthetic point of view is another matter.... Whatever the ultimate decision of the government, he would have to bow to the senators in the end.*

1955

In January, the impartial engineering firm's report results were announced by Park Service director Wirth. The findings substantiated the earlier government survey that claimed the shaft was structurally capable of supporting Hansen's new figure. The basic conclusion was that the shaft was safe for years to come and was presently capable of withstanding 20 percent more wind pressure than the strongest winds ever encountered in the area.

Scaffolding around monument column, September 1956. *NPS Photo.*

There was a recommendation that the monument's capital be replaced, anchoring the new figure with a steel rod with the lightning apparatus, re-pointing with mortar various crevices and cracks in the entire length of the tower and a rigid maintenance and inspection every five years.[106]

Hansen was given another one-year extension on his contract while the Park Services arranged for funding and execution of the reported recommendations. At first, Hansen's comments on the report were demure, as he had stated in public that he would abide by the findings. After a brief lull, he again broadcasted his usual protests against the soundness of the shaft, criticizing the interior rod and cable anchor system recommended and bemoaning the disregard for "esthetic" soundness.

Hansen brought forth a new argument, that of the size of his sculpture. He and his attorney lobbied the cast of sympathetic congress members to his cause. His figure turned out larger and heavier than what was contracted, and he blamed requested and approved changes by the Park Service. Portrayed as the starving and suffering artist, Hansen claimed to have spent $129,000 of his own money on the project and only received $33,067 to date from the government.[107]

A better time to ask for more money could not have been chosen, as the committees were appropriating funds for the Interior Department's 1956 projects in relation to preparations for the 1957 Jamestown 350th Anniversary. The fete would not be as grand or as many months long as the famed 1907 exposition, but it would shine a national and international spotlight on the park. After all, the queen was coming. Representative Jensen and Senator Robertson, after conferring with Director Wirth, included a $100,000 item in the funds for the National Park Service. Hansen would be paid $159,000 for his work.[108]

1956

At last, Hansen completed his statue of *Liberty*. In January, Superintendent Abbott and Elbert Cox, director of Region 1 of the National Park Service, visit the studio to inspect the work and make a report for Secretary McKay, who would make the decision to accept the work on behalf of the United States. Hansen referred to the work as "conceived to have meaning for everyone in the United States—an expression of whatever is benevolent, generous and noble in the female character we have adopted as a symbol of liberty."

And though Hansen bemoaned to the press that the money would cover only his out-of-pocket expenses, he said: "I am proud to have given over six years of my life to the cause of Liberty."[109]

On January 18, Secretary McKay officially accepted Hansen's statue. Per the terms of the contract, the figure had to be moved from the studio within thirty days. The Park Service used $15,000 from the 1954 appropriation to fund the contract to move the eleven-ton figure from the mountaintop studio in Charlottesville to Yorktown. A crane hoisted the two sections of the figure through the roof opening of Hansen's studio. From his rooftop perch, Hansen kissed the outreached hand of the figure before it was swung away to be loaded on trucks for the journey.

On February 24, *Liberty* arrived in Yorktown, under the care of the moving contractor E.T. Gresham Jr. of Norfolk. The statue was delivered in two pieces to the utility and supply yard of the Park Service, there placed under protective wraps and barricaded until the day it would be lifted to its perch on top of the monument.

But no sooner had the figure arrived and the Park Service began preparations for the installation than the subject of building a new shaft

Hansen's *Lady Liberty*, 1956. *From the Douglas and Mabel McKay Papers, OSU Libraries Special Collections & Archives Research Center.*

for the figure rose again. Hansen never ceased complaining about the shaft during any appearance or interview he gave, using his softer and charming persona to win over social groups as he had done with the DAR and others. Now his acquaintances in the Charlottesville unit of the American Association of University Women and the Albemarle County Historical

Oskar Hansen delivers photo album to Secretary of the Interior Douglas McKay. *From the Douglas and Mable Mckay Papers, OSU Libraries Special Collections & Archives Research Center.*

Society supported a campaign to have Virginia's congressional delegation support a new shaft suitable for Hansen's work.[110] Hansen sent Secretary McKay an album of photos of his new figure and pleaded his case once more for a new shaft elsewhere on the battlefield to hold his work. He was confident that the Park Service would not be able to accomplish the work to make the shaft suitable. Secretary McKay asked Director Wirth and Superintendent Abbott to "consider" looking further into the matter as they collected bids for the shaft work.

Bids for the repair work opened in April, and the winning bid was submitted by the John Daniels Company of Danville, Virginia. Their bid of $32,734 would encompass cutting a new pedestal stone, drilling a four-inch diameter hole through that stone and the entire shaft. A prestress cable was to be implanted in the cavity to prevent further deterioration and a lightning rod system—its topmost portion concealed from ground view by the aluminum headdress of the figure—installed. The entire structure was cleaned and given a protective coat of water repellant; scars and damages repaired. Removing the old figure and installing the new work was expected to take five months.

Above: Crane attempting to raise *Victory* figure from column, May 1956. *NPS Photo.*

Opposite: Removing *Victory* figure from column, May 1956. *NPS Photo.*

E.T. GRESHAM Co. INC.

Scaffolding once again went up around the monument, and a crane arrived to lower the old statue from its perch. But *Victory* did not give up its station willingly. While the remainder of the top section, which weighed only one ton, was easily removed as designed, the lower half put up a seven-hour fight, to the surprise of most everyone, with the exception of the onlooking DeNeufville. He had warned the work crew that the anchoring rod was twelve feet deep into the shaft. Even though the 1884 plans they were studying listed a pin of "gun metal" anchoring the statue, DeNeufville, who witnessed the installation, said it was made of brass. The crane was able to raise the lady's lower half only a few inches; with more prying, the base was wedged enough to access the pin. Unfortunately, they had planned for an iron or steel bolt and were using an acetylene cutting rig. After an hour, the foreman gave up on this method and declared the pin was indeed brass. After some conferring, the workmen concluded that in 1884 "gun metal" must have meant brass and a new saw was configured that ultimately cut through the pin.[111] After years of Oskar Hansen's vile tirades against the lady and the column's soundness, the construction proved true—the column did not collapse with the sculpture's removal.

What remained of J.Q.A. Ward's 1884 sculpture of *Victory* would not be honored for the fifty-eight years of patriotic awe it had stirred in the hearts of onlookers. To historians and art lovers alike, it was a bitter disappointment reading reports of *Victory* being broken up into chunks and its granite used to repair damages to the shaft, but in this way, at least Lady *Victory* will always live on at Yorktown.

Once *Victory* was removed from the shaft, drilling and installation of the interior pre-stress support cable and the lightning-protective system began on the column. The tunneling operations at the rear of the monument also began to anchor the pre-stress cable twenty inches below the base. Underground arrestor terminals installed at the base would extend one hundred feet in four directions. A core was drilled though the figure from foot to head, where the topmost portions of the lightning rod system would be concealed by the aluminum headdress in the fashion of a liberty cap and crown of laurel leaves.[112]

After 175 years, Benjamin Franklin finally contributed to the design of the Yorktown Monument that he promised Livingston, through the use of his invention: the lightning rod.

Lowering torso section to the ground, May 1956. *NPS Photo.*

Aluminum headdress with lightning rod. *NPS Photo.*

September 7 saw the square pedestal stone hoisted to the top of the shaft; this would be the support for the new lady atop the column.

On September 10, operators from the Moore Crane Company of Richmond began the process of raising the lower half of the new statue skyward. Breathless onlookers and a delegation from the Park Service and Washington, D.C., watched as the piece slowly rose into the air. Once the bottom was secured to the pedestal, the top half of the figure was lifted. With the sculpture's outstretched arms, this was a more delicate operation, yet both pieces arrived safely at the top courtesy of the crane operator's skill. To be safe, the Moore Company took out a one-day insurance policy of $150,000. With the figure secured in place, the Daniel Company continued with its pointing, patching and cleanup of the entire shaft, sandblasting the stone to remove stains and scars. The Stinchfield granite once again sparkled in the sun.

Through October, site work continued, but operations were not complete in time for the October observances. The various military, civic, social and international groups had to make do on the grounds of the Moore House that year. A formal dedication was scheduled for the following year to cap off the 1957 Jamestown anniversary celebration.

Oskar Hansen visited during the Yorktown Day commemorations to make his final inspection of the monument. The Park Service left the scaffolding in place for his use. Hansen, however, declined to climb the ladders and instead

Above: Raising *Liberty*'s top section. *NPS Photo.*

Left: *Liberty* figure installed atop column, October 1956. *NPS Photo.*

Liberty figure during installation, September 1956. *NPS Photo.*

studied the work from the ground using his field glasses. This also allowed him to interact with visitors and bask in their compliments on his work. When asked about his initial impressions, Hansen stated:

> *It's a bit too early to know what my final impressions will be…There is nothing that I could have done better…I think you'll find, that the whole monument has taken on a new significance.*

The installation complete, artist Oskar J.W. Hansen moved on to more lofty projects like creating "world peace." He announced at the end of the year that he would create and donate a communion chalice worth $1.5 million as a gift to promote peace, for nations to compete for annually. He also spent time in Washington, lobbing and testifying as a private citizen against President Eisenhower's Middle East policies.

1957

The October observance in 1957 capped off a hectic and prolific year for the State of Virginia and the Park Service. The Jamestown 350th Anniversary shone a national spotlight on the area and all its potential for development as a historical tourist mecca. The Park Service completed the Colonial Parkway connecting Yorktown, Williamsburg and Jamestown in time for the events. What the state had planned to be temporary exposition grounds, the Festival Park, proved to be a potential new revenue generator and plans developed for a permanent park as an added attraction to the National Park and the works of the APVA on Jamestown Island. During the celebration, the Queen of England, Elizabeth II, visited the site of the first permanent English settlement in the New World. Her itinerary, however, did not include a visit to the site of the decisive British defeat on the fields of Yorktown twenty-three miles away. Her visit generated publicity and tourist traffic to the area for years to come.

On October 19, the formal rededication of the monument was officiated by Secretary of the Army Wilbur M. Brucker and French ambassador Hervé Alphand. In the company of honored guests—descendants of French and American heroes—a crowd of 2,500 was regaled with oratory on the united front against Communism and the enduring alliance honored by the monument. For the first time in fifteen years, a lofty noble lady stood watch over all the events. Oskar Hansen was on hand, drawing his usual attention as he complained about the plaque to be installed at the monument, taking issue with the historical facts and verbiage. In this he was correct; signage states the monument was made of granite only from Hallowell, Maine. With the addition of the new *Liberty* figure, the monument now contains four different granites: Virginia stone in the foundation, Maine stone for the base and column, Rhode Island stone from *Victory* used for patch work and the North Carolina stone for the new lady.

Recognition block. *Photo by Devery Becker Jones, February 26, 2021, courtesy HMdb.org.*

Hansen also ensured that the monument would be properly titled for eternity by requiring that an inscription be etched into the first course of the stone base, called the "recognition block":

> *MONUMENT TO THE ALLIANCE AND VICTORY*
> *YORKTOWN MONUMENT COMMISSIONERS, 1881*
> *R.M. HUNT, ARCHITECT, CHAIRMAN*
> *HENRY VAN BRUNT, ARCHITECT*
> *J.Q.A. WARD, SCULPTOR*
> *OSKAR J.W. HANSEN, SCULPTOR OF* LIBERTY, *1957*

In the last decade of his life, Oskar Hansen saw his place as an Art Deco icon fade and his fame grow for his work on the *Liberty* statue. Hansen was a continual fixture in Washington, testifying as a concerned citizen against wars and foreign policy, then waging his own battles with the IRS. In 1958–59, he was at odds with the IRS, which claimed he did not pay income tax on the monies received for his work on the monument. Hansen appealed to the Senate, requesting adjustments to the appropriation due to his financial losses on the project. After several hearings on the matter, legislation was adjusted by Representative Jensen, with language stating: "That the intention in providing $100,000 in the 1956 act, was to compensate him, not for his services, but for the economic loss incurred by him on the project."[113]

Hansen continued his love-hate relationship with the National Park Service when he accepted a commission sponsored by the North Electric Company of Gallion, Ohio, to create busts of Wilbur and Orville Wright to be placed at the Wright Memorial at Kitty Hawk, North Carolina.

In 1963, Hansen sold his Pantops estate yet retained lifetime rights to his home and studio. Free from most of his debts, he then worked on various

Oskar Hansen poses with his Wright brothers sculptures. *From* This Old Palette *Blog, June 22, 2007, Chris Miller.*

projects such as cultivating his exotic plants and using them as models for small accent pieces that became hallmarks of the Virginia Metal Crafters Company.

Continuing his relationship with the U.S. government, in 1968 Hansen gifted the navy a bronze bust cast from the Yorktown *Liberty* statue. Standing over nine feet tall on its pedestal, the bust was displayed on the quarterdeck of the first nuclear carrier, USS *Enterprise*. The formal presentation at the Pentagon appeared to surprise the usually gregarious artist, who said: "I had no idea it would be such an elegant affair, a good handshake would have been enough for me."

Hansen revealed in conversations that he always considered the Yorktown Monument his "special" favorite, above even his winged figures at Hoover Damn.[114]

Oskar Hansen passed away in 1971 at the age of seventy-nine. Though his career and persona cannot be wholly judged by his years working on the Yorktown Monument, we can only take him at his own words: "I consider myself fortunate that I have two things of permanent record—the Boulder Dam figures, which give meaning to engineering, and Liberty at Yorktown, where the constitutional process began."[115]

Hansen experienced at Yorktown what so many before him had and in some way or another still do. He felt the heart-pounding patriotic awe of the place and history that surrounded him, accompanied by the bitter disappointment that everyone did not share his artistic vision.

Notes on Allegories

J.Q.A. Ward's *Victory* embodied all the classic traditions of the personification of American ideas, hearkening back to those Greek statues. With its sandaled foot and bare leg extended behind a slim, sheer-clad form, outstretched bare arms, long neck and upswept hair, the sculpture could have embodied any of the founding ideals. The original design presented an allegory of Liberty wearing the Phrygian cap of freedom crowned with stars and holding the nation's shield in one hand, the other outreached offering the blessing of freedom. The finished statue was a strange departure from that plan, without the shield and the figure's arms raised. The change was interpreted by some as a motion of blessing or calming, by others as a gesture of victory. With the only symbolic element being the Phrygian cap, symbolizing freedom and the pursuit of liberty, is where the confusion of the title began. Is it *Victory* or *Liberty*? While the crowning figure was never formally titled by the sculptor, the report by the commission of artists in 1881 conveying the emblematic significance of the monument states:

> *This monument is intended to convey—that by the victory at Yorktown, the independence of the United States of America was achieved.... The column, thus adorned, culminates with Liberty herself, star-crowned, and welcoming the people of all nations to share equally with us the fruits of our peace and prosperity.*

First and foremost, the monument as a whole was a memorial to the alliance with the French and the victory at Yorktown. The lady on top went by any name that came first to the mind of the onlooker. Some saw *Victory*, some saw *Liberty*. The locals just called her "Miss Yorktown,"

Oskar Hansen did title his figure *Liberty*, yet his interpretation departs from the usual depiction of the personification of Liberty. The founding fathers looked toward the classical periods and the genesis of democracy in Greece and Rome to visually express the ideas that would influence the new nation's architecture in its capitol and symbols of its ideals. Ancient-winged Victory; Nike and Roma; Themis or "Justice," the blindfolded lady with her scales; and Libertas or "Liberty" were all usually portrayed as a classic Greek goddess, toga-clad, sandal-shod, upswept hair laurel-crowned, immune to modesty as she charged, often bare breasted, leading the nation. Toward the Civil War era, Liberty became more Victorian,

Allegory of Freedom 1788, printmaker Christian Bernhard Rode. *Art World/Almay Stock.*

with long flowing hair and more modern dress. This finally culminated in the ultimate expression of Liberty in the New York Harbor, the image that now comes first to mind for all Americans.

The image Hansen created, rather than an expression of Liberty through an unrestrained female form, would be more at home in a church niche, behind an altar or set in a memorial garden. To this day, onlookers at Yorktown mistake the *Liberty* figure for the Virgin Mary. The only flesh exposed on Hansen's *Liberty* is head and hands; the figure is heavily cloaked

THE GODDESS OF LIBERTY.

Opposite: The Goddess of Liberty, circa 1865. *Library of Congress.*

Left: Statue of Liberty, New York Harbor, from the south, circa 1891. *Library of Congress.*

and even wearing sensible shoes, which contributed to the statue being larger and heavier than the original. Hansen explained:

> *In the preliminary discussions about the design of the new "Liberty", with two Park Service chiefs it was agreed the old figure had certain anatomical abnormalities...the out-stretched foot extended backwards, which the lightning also hit. A new composition was agreed upon. You know what a lady does with her legs, she never crosses them, or unduly exposes them.*[116]

The only homage paid to the classic feminine allegory is the sheer blouse that covers the figure's detailed breasts. Hansen explained his sculpture's composition as a welcoming gesture of Liberty that symbolizes readiness to give with one hand and to bless with the other. Aesthetically, however,

View of *Liberty* from the ground. *Courtesy of Linda Williams.*

Hansen believed that his larger figure put sufficient mass and volume at the top to pull the base back into proportion. He also coordinated the flow of Liberty's cloak with the ornaments up the shaft so that the ornateness is subdued. Here is where much credit is due to Hansen; here is where his artistic genius shines through all the egotistical bluster. He designed his lady with the knowledge that it would not be viewed head on but gazed upon by those looking up from one hundred feet below.

Part IV

Bicentennial

"Commemorations and Aspirations"

Liberty was now aloft and firmly planted on the long-berated column. *The Monument to Alliance and Victory* was whole again and continued its dominance over the landscape of Yorktown, drawing visitors' gazes and patriotic spirits upward. The October observances in Yorktown ebbed and flowed from year to year, based on current events that affected the community or the country—some years grand, some more subdued. A collage of competing events sponsored by various history, civic, social and military interests were regular occurrences. The event of 1960 featured speaker Dr. Tench Francis Tilghman, descendant of Washington's aide, continuing that family's association with Yorktown.

Though the monument was part of the Colonial National Historical Park, it had become the complete identity of the town and the County of York. In 1969, York County adopted a seal and flag that featured the monument as first erected.[117] For those who lived and worked in the county, the monument was an official identity—it was incorporated into every government department's logo and displayed on licenses, deeds, diplomas, tax stickers and police and fire vehicles. For schoolchildren in York County, the battlefield and the monument were yearly field trips for all grades. York County and its neighbor James City County were a rural buffer between the industrial cities of Richmond to the north and Norfolk to the south. After the completion of the Colonial Parkway through the heart of both counties and Colonial Williamsburg in 1957, these rural areas saw a new growth in tourism, which would become their dominant industry.

Above: Park rangers hang memorial wreath during Yorktown Day observance. *U.S. Air Force Photo/Staff. Sgt. Wesley Farnsworth.*

Left: Seal of York County, Virginia.

York County continued to be rural and agrarian with no centralized urban center of commerce. The village of Yorktown, laid out in 1691 on fifty acres divided into one hundred lots plus the common waterfront, was, however, the seat of government. The colonial-style courthouse and jail built in 1955 on the same lot as the first 1700s court, with a few administrative office buildings, was the meeting place of the board of supervisors. Never "incorporated" as a town, the area was overseen by a board of trustees consisting of local business owners and residents. Yorktown's one hundred lots were now a patchwork of private, county and National Park Service ownership, with boundaries and property rights in constant dispute.

The National Park Service had a delicate relationship with its neighbors in the town. The original "master plan" for the park in the 1930s was to incorporate the entire village into the park and restore and reconstruct the 1700s village, with a portion of the waterfront offering interpretation similar to what evolved at Colonial Williamsburg. But the grand master plan ran afoul of county government and local residents. Even more debilitating to the plan were the Great Depression and the constant federal budget cuts to the Park Service each year, which did not allow for a swift and complete consolidation of properties in the beginning of the park's development. Over the years, the park slowly acquired properties to incorporate into the battlefield preservation. The Monument Lodge, a thirty-room hotel built in 1925 by the Renforth family only a few steps from the monument grounds, was acquired by the Park Service in 1961 through a land exchange with the family. The hotel was razed in order to provide a clear view of Main Street from the park's new visitor's center, which was built on the site of the failed Manor Hotel and Country Club. The removal also allowed further study and archaeology into the last few acres of the Secretary Nelson Plot.[118] In 1968, the Park Service acquired the Nelson House and all the town lots that George Preston Blow had amassed in the early 1900s during that heyday of speculation from the heirs of the Blow family. The third generation no longer wished to reside in the area yet sought to continue their family's tradition of contributing to the preservation of historic properties and offered the estate to the Park Service.[119] The house and grounds that Kate Nelson once offered to the government for $2,500, as a residence for a monument keeper in 1884, would now cost $777,000, the appraised value of all the properties. The Park Service then began a five-year project to restore the house to its original pre–Revolutionary War condition, removing all the modern amenities and renovations installed over the years by the Blow family. The goal was to have the house ready for public tours and interpretation by the time of the national bicentennial in 1976.

The yearlong national celebration of America's bicentennial was like a never-ending Fourth of July event in Yorktown. In May of that year, the president of France, Valery Giscard d'Estaing, and his entourage, accompanied by Governor Mills Godwin, visited the monument quietly and unannounced. The party observed the inscriptions and plaques and placed a gigantic bouquet of white roses on the steps before pulling off in the motorcade. July 4 and Yorktown Day in October were bigger and more exciting than the usual observances. Tourism in the area increased as people came to visit the battlefield to get in touch with their country's history. Everything that was American in general was celebrated. Americans expressed their identity in the symbols of Minute Men soldiers, bald eagles, flags and images of the founding fathers and the Declaration of Independence. Yorktown had its symbolic monument, which filled the hearts of onlookers with patriotic awe when illuminated by fireworks on summer evenings. Yet bitter disappointment would lie ahead for some Americans who called Yorktown "home."

In line with the long-range plan leading to Yorktown's own bicentennial in 1981 would be the relocation of the remaining residents of Union Town or "Slab Town," the community built during the Civil War by the formerly enslaved who had fled to the protection of Union forts and were declared "contraband." With congressional funding, this community that had grown up in sight of the monument on the outskirts of Yorktown proper would be bought out by the government. Those residents who resisted the government's financial offers had their property condemned by eminent domain.[120] Once the residents were relocated and the structures removed, those land parcels were incorporated into the battlefield, where archaeology and fortification restoration would commence—a community sacrificed for the sake of preservation. This was one of the many ironies of the Yorktown story: early residents wanted the trenches and fortifications torn down for the benefit of the community, while residents of Slab Town saw their community torn down for the benefit of the fortifications and trenches.

The 1976 bicentennial set off over a decade of ultra-patriotic events that would highlight the "Historic Triangle," as Jamestown, Williamsburg and Yorktown were becoming known and marketed. During this time, the State of Virginia entered the history tourism game again by establishing in Yorktown an exhibition museum to be called the Victory Center. Virginia learned after the 1957 Jamestown fete that there was revenue to be had by promoting Virginia's history, and tourism was becoming a competitive industry for the region. The state had already transformed its temporary exposition at Jamestown, the Festival Park, into a permanent attraction, with its replicas of ships, fort and Indian village. The Victory Center at Yorktown would be its sister museum to carry on the colonial and Revolution story. In Yorktown, the Victory Center overlapped the interpretation of the National Park, yet the two coexist. In the middle was the town; with a National Park Battlefield on one side and the new museum on the other, it hoped to profit from both. In these years of patriotic tourism, the monument was a focal point for any occasion, commemoration or photo-op.

Modern heroes pay tribute to the Battle of Yorktown. *U.S. Air Force Photo/Staff Sgt. Christina M. Styer.*

Continuing the theme of patriotism, in 1980 America hosted the Winter Olympics. The sun-kindled flame from Athens, Greece, arrived in America at Langley Air Force Base. From there, its bearer took a twenty-one-mile boat ride up the York River and arrived at the wharf to great fanfare. A parade of fifty-two state representatives chosen to run the Olympic torch arrived at the monument. There, in a brief ceremony, in the middle of the coldest, snowiest day to date in the area, people in attendance were allowed to light candles from the sacred flame before it began its journey to Lake Placid, New York. From the steps of the Yorktown Victory Monument, the first torchbearer set off.[121]

Preparations for Yorktown's bicentennial began on a grander scale than that of the national bicentennial five years before. The celebration called for grand commemorations and even grander memorials, and just as during the sesquicentennial, more bronze plaques and tablets throughout the town and perhaps a new monument to the anniversary could be erected. But as the story of Yorktown's Victory Monument illustrates, erecting and maintaining monuments are not easy feats. The itinerary of the usual yearly commencements was produced by the usual loose affiliation of various groups: Daughters and Sons of the Revolution, Society of the Cincinnati, various local history groups, the Association for the Preservation of Virginia Antiquities, Page-Nelson Society, Yorktown Trustees, National Park Service, Military Associations, Historical Re-enactors and international "Friends" societies. The bicentennial committee, however, in addition to those groups, was the concern of state and local governments, with federal organizations facilitating the visit of President Ronald Reagan, French president François Mitterrand and other international delegations. Yorktown at two hundred would have an anniversary on par with any of the previous Jamestown celebrations.

The Lafayette-Rochambeau Society of Washington, a group dedicated to paying tribute to French veterans of the Revolution—and regular attendees of the Yorktown Day observances, sponsors of the marble cross and plaque placed at the French Cemetery on the Battlefield—suggested that the present Victory Monument was also a centennial monument. Another should be raised to mark the second hundred years and continue at each century observance. Twenty years prior to the bicentennial, that organization's director, while attending a dinner in Paris, met the renowned artist Felix de Weldon, sculptor of the Iwo Jima Memorial at Arlington National Cemetery. De Weldon was asked and agreed to create a model of a possible monument for the society to place at Yorktown. After years that saw no

Plaster cast model of the three generals, the Proposed Yorktown Bicentennial Monument by Felix de Weldon, 1981. *NPS Photo.*

momentum on the project, de Weldon decided at the last minute to take on the task himself. With only twenty-four months until the 1981 celebration, de Weldon conceived a work almost as massive as his World War II opus. It was a bronze relief depicting the generals—Washington, Rochambeau and Lafayette—on horseback, twenty-six feet tall and forty-two feet long against a marble wall with an etched granite tablet depicting French ships in the Chesapeake Bay and tribute to Admiral de Grasse. A second tablet with the narrative of the battle would be inscribed in both English and French. At his own expense of $230,000, he constructed the clay model and a plaster casting of his proposed monument.

Two weeks prior to the October 19 observance, three trucks arrived at Surrender Field in Yorktown, hauling the thirty pieces of the plaster model. It took six days to assemble the temporary monument, seal it with a waterproof coating and then paint it with a faux bronze patina. William Petsco, a foundry worker from New York who had been aide to de Weldon since the 1954 Iwo Jima project, and a small crew worked nonstop to assemble the work for presentation. Removing the last of the scaffolding only ten minutes before the ceremonies, Petsco barely had time to change clothes and take his seat before the American and French anthems began to play.[122] The model was to be on display during the days of the bicentennial and through mid-December for visitors to see and to help drum up donations to the project. De Weldon and groups that supported the project hoped for a goal of $750,000, along with the tentative cooperation and blessing of the Park Service to allow the privately funded monument to be placed on federal land.

On Sunday, October 18, the French-American Monument Foundation held a ceremony to commemorate the French generals of the Revolutionary War. The event, designed by de Weldon, featured orations by various directors of historical associations, musical entertainment by the Continental Army Band and attendance by descendants of Revolutionary War generals and other officers who served at Yorktown.[123] The model stood at Surrender Field only until mid-November, when the remnants of a hurricane passed through the coastal areas, bringing wind gusts that blew over the model and cracked it into pieces. Felix de Weldon had the pieces collected and returned to his Washington, D.C. studio where it had been created to wait in storage until the funds for bronzing could be raised. After a few years that saw no organized funding for the project, and with the cost of bronzing now inflating to possibly $1 million, original supporters began to back away. The Bicentennial Committee could offer no help to the project; de Weldon had entered his monument too late in the planning and funding stages of the event. All funds had been appropriated and distributed before his proposal, and there was no more state or county money to be added to a budget planned years in advance. All funds would have to be raised privately.

Mary Mathews, restaurant owner, Yorktown's most philanthropic patron and a member of the town trustees, tried to keep the project alive, suggesting they sell desk-size replicas of the monument for $1,000 each to raise funds, yet the county officials lost interest and backed out of the de Weldon project altogether. The outspoken Mathews scolded them all for having "no appreciation" of the importance of Yorktown.[124] Ten years later, when reached for comment by the press doing a follow-up story, Felix de Weldon said, "I am very anxious to complete this memorial. Since it commemorates the battle of Yorktown I think it should be in Yorktown….[It is] important because it thanks the French for their contribution to the victory."

In 1993, deep in debt after his wife's long illness, de Weldon was forced into bankruptcy and his studio and its contents of uncast models and works in various stages were sold piece by piece for the lowest fractions of their value. The plaster model of the Iwo Jima statue sold for only one hundred dollars.[125] The auction company, R.L. Rasmus of Alexandria, did not keep

Artist Felix de Weldon, circa 1985. *Courtesy U.S. Marine Corps History Division.*

records of the event's transactions, so it can only be assumed that someone, somewhere purchased a piece if not all of the clay or the plaster casting of the forgotten proposed Yorktown Bicentennial Monument.

The 1981 event brought a new light to the monument. The large floodlights that had bathed the monument in light since the sesquicentennial were removed during World War II as a defense effort. Since that time, it had stood in darkness. Mathews had suggested relighting the monument to the trustees earlier in the year, and the county Ruritans Club took up the project to raise donations to create a perpetual fund that would pay the electric bill. Lights similar to those that illuminate the Washington Monument and the Statue of Liberty were donated by the Crouse-Hinds Company. On October 12, as part of the Yorktown Day Observances, the re-lighting ceremony was held. After forty years, the monument was once again bathed in light. Speeches and the Tactical Air Command Band marked the occasion. Lines read from the poem "Independence Was Won" by Cornelius Tate set the tone:

> *No more in darkness will I stand, on this quiet and peaceful land. By day the sun will shine so bright, and the "Lights of Freedom" will shine by.*[126]

Every October, after a year of community BBQ sales and other fundraising projects, the Ruritans Club presents the Park Service superintendent with a check to keep the lights on the monument for another year.

The 1984 Fourth of July brought to Yorktown its new namesake, the fifth incarnation of the USS *Yorktown*, carrying on that name after a sloop of war, a gunboat and two aircraft carriers. The guided missile cruiser (CG-48) was commissioned at the Yorktown Naval Weapons Station on July 4 and then docked at Yorktown to join the festivities as a feature attraction of the holiday celebrations. A cake topped with a five-foot, six-inch confectionary replica of the monument was the highlight of an early birthday salute to the landmark. The years of ultra-patriotic celebrations concluded with the 1984 October observance marking the one hundredth anniversary of the Yorktown Victory Monument's completion.

The October observance of 1989 corrected an omission long advocated for by Franco-American societies since the sesquicentennial. During the 1981 bicentennial, it was noted by French veterans' organizations that though there was a cross and plaque that denoted the site of an unmarked common grave of some fifty French soldiers, nowhere were the names of the fallen inscribed in memorial as per the French custom. The ambassador of France to the United States M. Emmanuel de Margerie appointed the Committee for the Yorktown French Memorial, a committee of both French and American members with the goal to erect a memorial to honor those soldiers and sailors who had given their lives during the Yorktown siege and the naval "Battle of the Capes." This group was charged with the design, approval, funding and dedication of the memorial. Private donations to the project totaled $60,000. The result was a wall of curved granite, six feet tall

Guided missile cruiser, USS *Yorktown* (CG48), July 4, 1984. *U.S. National Archives.*

and seventeen feet wide, inscribed with six hundred known names of the regular soldiers and sailors, erected at the location of a French defensive work from the battle overlooking the river. After eight years, the dedication was held during the observance of 1989, attended by a crowd of three hundred, including French veterans' groups, the French Ninety-Ninth Regiment, units of reenactors, descendant groups and historical societies, and officiated by the French ambassador and the National Park Service.

In 1990, the new year and the new decade brought new ironies to the story of Yorktown's Monument. It was a bad year in general for monuments in the area. In May, the National Park Service in the Capitol Region was struggling with the deterioration of many of Washington, D.C's monolithic monuments from pollution, acid rain and visitors. The smooth marble finishes were becoming pitted and stained. There were problems with mortar and caulking, and structures were plagued by drainage problems, corrosion and asbestos. Even the cleaning regimes were contributing to the rapid deterioration of the marble, creating a conundrum for the Park Service's maintenance division.

Monument to the Soldiers and Sailors of the French Expeditionary Force. *Author's collection.*

> *It is well documented that the American public expects to find these national treasures in a pristine state when they visit.*[127]

In Yorktown, on the night of Saturday, June 30, forty-eight years after lightning struck the figure of *Victory*, it struck once again at *Liberty*. The next morning, a tourist walked into the Park Service office carrying pieces of the lady's severed left hand found on the ground. Inspections showed that *Liberty* had suffered the loss of its left hand, fingers on the right, cracks to the face and chin and possibly a fracture to the torso. The park and town had to scramble on the eve of the Fourth of July to rearrange all the events planned around the monument for the public's safety. The usual launching site for the fireworks display was moved for fear the vibration would further damage the monument, a disappointment to the crowd of five thousand who had chosen prime viewing seats around the monument grounds.[128] By the first of October, the Carving and Restoration Team of Manassas had arrived to remove the top section of the statue, conduct repairs to the cracks and sculpt a new hand, reassembling the monument in time for the October

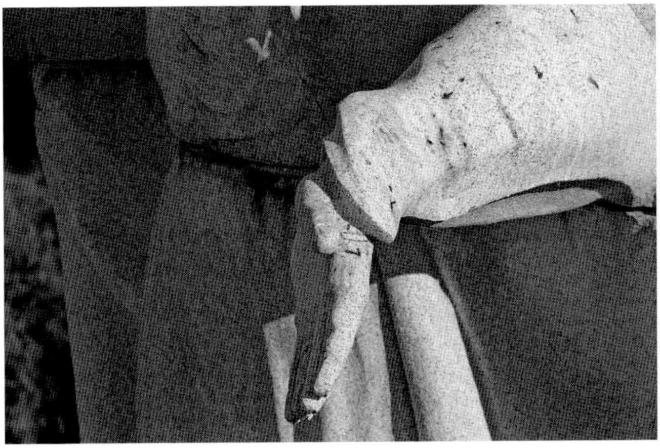

Close-up of replaced hand. *NPS Photo.*

observance. The new hand lacked the grace of the original but kept to the guidelines of historic preservation and restoration—not to reinterpret the original but maintain its stability.

Reflecting on all the criticism Oskar Hansen had heaped on *Victory*'s design and style and the ridicule for it only lasting fifty-eight years, touting the superiority and longevity of his own work, one can't help but imagine that the sculptor J.Q.A. Ward would be amused to see that Hansen's "superior" design had held up for only thirty-four years. Not even the addition of five lightning rods could protect Hansen's work from the whims of nature.

Liberty was refreshed and restored and ready for 1991, when the Town of York would celebrate its 300th anniversary. Established in 1691 by the Ports Act, the area was chosen to become an official trade port, collecting his majesty's tariffs and taxes on import and exports. The deep river and natural harbor made the town of fifty acres on the bluff and the common shore below the trading capital of the region. For three days in August, the various history groups, local folks and visiting tourists celebrated the area's colonial heyday before the Revolution with costume parades, entertainments, plays, concerts and tours of the historic buildings of the town. The Tercentennial Committee hoped the celebration would showcase what Yorktown had to offer visitors who were absorbed by Williamsburg and Jamestown.[129] The October observance for this year also commemorated the 210th anniversary of the Battle of Yorktown, officiated by French ambassador Jacques Andreani on the stage at the monument's base.

In 1994, plans were put in motion for another monument to keep *Liberty* company on Main Street. The French had their monument to the war dead; now the York County Historical Committee sought to honor its

Park rangers hang the memorial wreath during Yorktown Day ceremonies. *NPS Photo.*

own residents who had served and were lost throughout all of America's wars. Researchers Rose Schatzel and Tim Smith collected names of those county residents to be memorialized on a simple granite pylon, a miniature of the Washington Monument measuring seven feet.[130] They chose the grounds of the York County Court House at the end of Main Street, with hopes of erecting the monument by 1996 at a cost of $12,000. But this is Yorktown, and monuments don't come quick or within budget. During the years of fundraising, York County moved its courthouse from the site it had occupied since the 1700s to the location of the new County Government Complex on the edge of the village. The 1955 Colonial-style building on Main Street became an art gallery and county museum. The committee felt that the proper place for the monument was the historic location of the original courthouse, where visitation would be greater. It was 2001 before the monument was installed and dedicated on Memorial Day at a cost of $25,000 from private donations. The names of 106 county residents from Bacon's Rebellion to the Vietnam War are inscribed on the four sides of the obelisk; 26 additional names are planned from the more recent Wars on Terror.

York County War Memorial. *Photo by Bernard Fisher, May 30, 2015, courtesy HMdb.org.*

The new millennium brought with it new anniversary observances. While Colonial Williamsburg celebrated its 300th anniversary in 1999, planning was in motion for the 225th Yorktown Day in 2006, to be followed by the Jamestown 400th in 2007. The monument stood timeless above Yorktown as the dawning light of a new century shimmered over the waters of the York River, quelling the fears of the unrealized Y2K electronic apocalypse. The next year, the monument was again an ultra-patriotic symbol while all the military bases in its radius marshaled their resources for war after the attacks of 9/11. For the next few years, the October observances again took on the sense of heightened national pride that had defined the bicentennial years.

The monument stood strong in September 2003 when Hurricane Isabelle struck the area with a force not seen since the 1933 storm, once again proving true the wind study done by the Corps of Engineers in 1883. The commercial waterfront below the monument grounds, however, was destroyed by the storm surge. A month of continuous rains had saturated the ground and weakened the root system of ages old trees in the area, toppling them in the winds. Infrastructure damage from Norfolk to Richmond left people without power and in some places contaminated drinking water for weeks. Falling trees uprooted graves in the National Cemetery, the Parkway was impassable, covered in downed trees, but Jamestown had suffered the most: when parts of the island were underwater, flooding the storage buildings housing the collection of artifacts and destroying the Park Service Visitor Center.

Yorktown's 225th celebration in 2006 saw an influx of military reenactors that rivaled the 1981 bicentennial. The four-day celebration featured the reenactment of various battles, artillery demonstrations and the surrender ceremony re-created step by step for a film crew. There were the usual orations, memorial wreath laying, commemorations and themed entertainments. It did, however, lack the star power of a head of state visit, the keynote speaker being the secretary of the interior and the French ambassador. That year saw a rebound in tourism; it had been in decline since 9/11. But Yorktown's anniversary, for all its pageantry, was overshadowed by the Jamestown event the next year. Once again, the resources of the National Park Service, the State of Virginia and the federal government were in play for the 400th anniversary. In the years since the hurricane, government agencies had used all available resources, disaster aid and appropriations to rebuild and expand Jamestown's facilities in time for the celebration—after all, the queen was coming again. Elizabeth II, after her visit fifty years before, returned to

Patrouille de France, the French Aerobatic Demonstration Team, performs a fly-over, October 8, 2009. *Courtesy of Mike Lynaugh.*

Rangers at attention during memorial observances. *NPS Photo.*

Jamestown for the celebration of the first permanent English colony in the New World. Just as during the monarch's last visit, Yorktown, the scene of British defeat in the New World, did not make it onto her itinerary.

In 2011, the monument was again tested by Mother Nature, as the Hampton Roads area experienced a 5.8-magnitude earthquake on August 23. Centered in Louisa County, Virginia, the effects were felt as far as Maine in the North and Georgia in the South. Not since 1897 had the area experienced such an event. Though there are no reports as to how the monument reacted in 1897, in 2011 the Victory Monument stood fast and suffered no ill effects.

As time marches on, in addition to the annual October observances, in a place so connected to historical events, there is always an anniversary to commemorate or an overlooked hero to acknowledge. The years 2011 through 2015 encompassed the various sesquicentennials of Civil War events throughout the National Battlefields and historic sites both North and South. Reenactors and enthusiasts descended on the locations of importance to the May 1862 Peninsular Campaign and the Union siege and occupation of Yorktown.

The Yorktown Victory Monument was erected twenty years after the end of the Civil War. It would be celebrated as the first national monument in

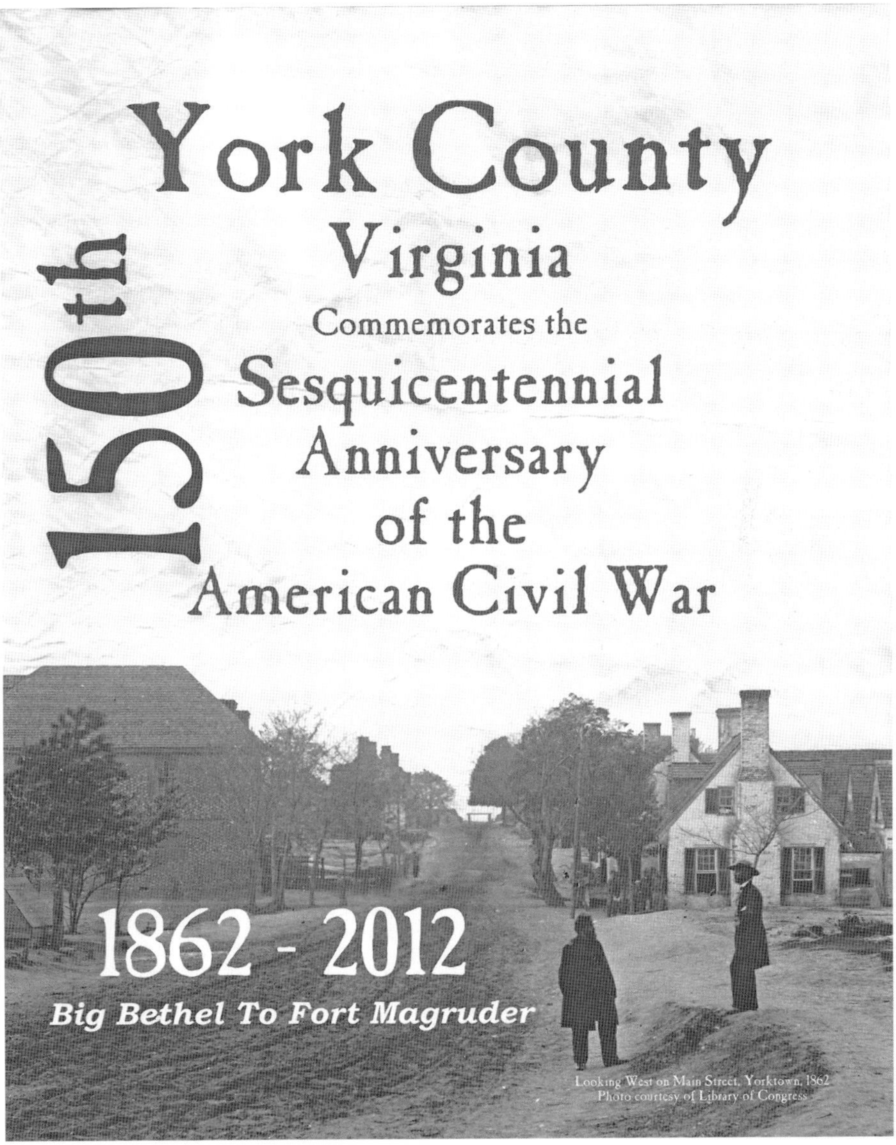

Program of activities for the York County Civil War Sesquicentennial. *The York County Sesquicentennial of the American Civil War Committee.*

the South to express a unified country's heritage and national identity, yet it was often referred to as the "Confederate Monument" by northern writers who never visited it for themselves. Those references gave the impression that it was simply another Civil War memorial like those in every populous city throughout the South. Yorktown's monument was often misidentified on maps, in brochures, in newspaper articles and on postcards as "The Soldiers Memorial," "The Surrender Monument," "The Liberty Monument," "The Veterans Monument," "The Peace Monument" and many other variations.

The Monument to Alliance and Victory at Yorktown is now most often identified by the shorter "Victory Monument," and the lady on top (courtesy of Oskar Hansen) is now always referred to as *Liberty*.

As a tribute to America's first war victory, the monument is a link to those who first took up arms in the cause of independence. Today, it welcomes those who would follow in the footsteps of those first citizen-soldiers. Members of each and every branch of military service visit the monument throughout the year. The Army Old Guard Fife & Drum Corp marches in the Yorktown Day parades. The Coast Guard Training School is located on the edge of the battlefield. Naval ships cruise past the monument on the waters of the York River en route to supply bases. The jets of Langley Field, as well as the impressive sight of Air Force One skimming the fields on its touch-and-go maneuvers, can be seen overhead. Honor Guards and security details of marines accompany diplomats and heads of state. Army

Close-up of the *Liberty* figure, October 28, 2017. *DrStew82, Wikimedia Commons.*

Service members and families honored with a new park pass providing free admission to all federal recreation lands, May 16, 2012. *U.S. Air Force Photo/Senior Airman John D. Strong II.*

staff rides, War College classes and regular soldiers, seamen and airmen all visit the battlefield, and the monument is their rallying point.

The year 2016 saw the one hundredth birthday of the National Park Service itself. Founded in 1916, the service evolved from taking care of America's natural wonders to include preserving America's history and culture. Colonial National Historical Park, encompassing the Yorktown Battlefield, Jamestown Island, Colonial Parkway and the monument, was among the Park Service's first endeavors into historic restoration and preservations. Throughout the year, the monument was the center of the park's outreach activities and events. National Park rangers are the caretakers and custodians of our collective memories and souvenirs, ensuring that we can learn from them and pass the history on.

The monument's story is almost as epic as the event it commemorates: its century-long journey to construction, the symbolism of the embellishments chosen to adorn it and the people who created and maintain it. Interpreting the story to visitors is a constant challenge for the park. Wayside markers are the current method of identifying landmarks, though it is preference and policy not to overshadow the landscape with signage. Markers are brief and often leave readers wanting more. The park's visitor center is a short stroll from the monument and the best place to start any history quest.

It has often been said that "monuments are for the living, not the dead."[131] The Victory Monument is the defining feature of Colonial National Historical Park. It is a landmark for traveling tourists and historic purists alike. It is an archive and history lesson about the nation's victory in the War for Independence. It is the avatar of a region's identity. It is a rallying point for the charitable cause and a cause célèbre. It is the touchstone for celebrated communal and personal achievements and victories. Runners and cyclists who start or end their cross-country journeys, school classes and sport teams,

Left: Ranger Stikeleather and Ranger Beck welcome visitors to the annual observances. *NPS Photo*.

Below: Monument interpretive marker. *Photo by Devery Becker Jones, February 26, 2021, courtesy HMdb.org.*

military service people being promoted or reenlisted, committed couples, newly made citizens, survivors of any struggle and many others choose the Yorktown Victory Monument as their witness and photo backdrop. It is the pillar of an outdoor cathedral that welcomes the faithful to Easter sunrise service and candlelight vigils, the communities to orchestral performances, joyous patriotic citizens who watch the skies explode with light and color and the artists of every medium who try to capture its spirit.

Scaffolding rose around the monument in 2018 for routine inspection and cleaning, after which discussions began about the lady's future. Her left hand, once again victim of the elements, was removed in 2016 for safety and to eliminate further damage. Following the assessments, the *Liberty* figure's soundness after so much exposure came into question.

As of this writing, the Park Service is consulting with preservation teams about the monument's future.[132] There is a consensus that the *Liberty* figure's integrity is rapidly declining, and it will need to be replaced. Studies and evaluations of historic preservation guidelines and engineering recommendations are in the long-term planning stages. Only time will tell if the powers that be will look to the past as a lesson in replacement should they opt for a new figure to be carved of granite and, if so, which, Victory or Liberty? How should such a figure be interpreted, Neo-classical, pre-Hellenic, Art Deco? How do we, in the twenty-first century, replace an element on a monument conceived in the eighteenth century, built in the nineteenth century and repaired in the twentieth? The architect Henry Van Brunt stated:

> [It is] *our duty to express with our art the civilization of our time.*[133]

Perhaps it is time to think outside of the box and consider something different. Perhaps taking a mold of the present lady and casting it in bronze or embracing new-age resins and composites used to preserve historic architecture that mimic stone to cast the figure might be an option. Maybe it will be a sculpture that resembles the original approved figure as shown in the architectural drawings. Whatever the solution, to be sure, it will be an *epic* task, years in the making.

It has been almost 250 years now since Lieutenant Colonel Tench Tilghman made his ride fresh from the victory on the field to deliver that news to Congress, and they then resolved to memorialize Yorktown with a marble column. Yorktown now stands itself as a monument among monuments as it approaches its semiquincentennial in 2031. The Victory Monument will

Victory Monument in summer. *Bill Coughlin, August 12, 2008, courtesy HMdb.org.*

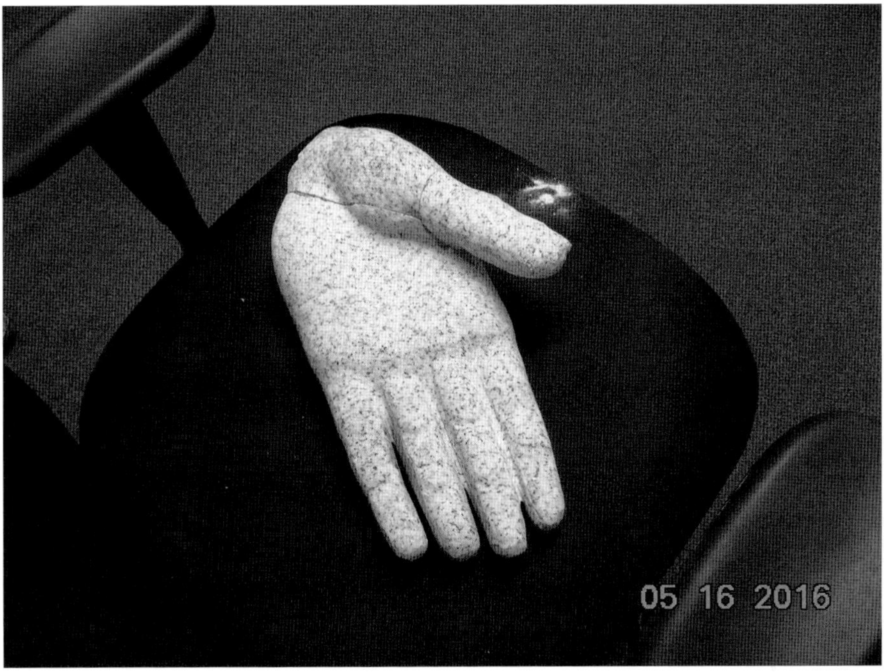

Damage to replacement hand, prompting removal in 2018. *NPS photo by Tim Mclean.*

Cracks through *Liberty*'s face and neck. *NPS Photo.*

"One Country, One Constitution, One Destiny." *Courtesy of Mike Lynaugh.*

mark its tercentennial celebration in 2081, which should indeed be a source of stirring patriotic awe if we can avoid the disappointment of forgetting why we ever wanted a monument in the first place.

> *May the Monument here to be erected be preserved throughout all ages as a reminder to each succeeding generation of the glorious event which it is intended to commemorate.*[134]

Notes

Part I

1. Harrison and Tilghman, *Memoir of Lieut. Col. Tench Tilghman.*
2. Rawle and Rawle, "Loyalist's Account."
3. Resolutions of Congress, meeting in Philadelphia, Monday, October 29, 1781.
4. Stevens, *Yorktown Centennial Handbook.*
5. Johnston, *Correspondence and Public Papers*, 3:417–18.
6. Jameson, "To Level the Works at York."
7. Hiden, "Losses of York County Citizens."
8. National Archives, Papers of the Continental Congress, No. 78, XIII, 285–88, https://catalog.archives.gov/id/1938489.
9. Library of Congress, Journals of the Continental Congress, 1774–1789 XXV, 533, https://catalog.loc.gov/vwebv/search?searchCode=LCCN&searchArg=05000059&searchType=1&permalink=y.
10. Weld, *Travels through the States.*
11. La Rochefoucauld-Liancourt and Neuman, *Travels through the United States.*
12. Latrobe, *Essay on Landscape.*
13. York County, Virginia, https://www.yorkcounty.gov/2386/Citizen-News-Weekly.
14. *Richmond Enquirer*, March 4, 1814.
15. Scott, *To the Public.*
16. Brandon, *Lafayette*, vol. 3, 57.

17. Ward, *Account of General La Fayette's Visit.*
18. *Gale and Seaton's Register of Debates.*
19. Folsom, "Yorktown in 1854."
20. Lossing, *Pictorial Field-book*, vol. 2.
21. Smith, *Old Yorktown.*
22. Ibid., 19.
23. Quoted in Stone, *Our French Allies.*
24. Emerging Civil War, "Battlefield Markers & Monuments: Yorktown Monument—A Victim of Another War," emergingcivilwar.com.
25. *Official Programme of the Yorktown Centennial Celebration.*
26. Ibid.
27. *Statutes at Large*, vol. 21, session 22, Forty-Sixth Congress, 163.
28. Stevens, *Yorktown Centennial Handbook.*
29. Senate Report No. 1003.
30. *Official Programme of the Yorktown Centennial Celebration.*
31. Yorktown Sesquicentennial Commission [hereafter YCC] and Bland, *Proceedings.*
32. YCC, *Report of the Commission.*
33. YCC and Bland, *Proceedings.*
34. Letter of Wm. P. Craighill to Robert T. Lincoln, Secretary of War, November 9, 1881.
35. YCC and Bland, *Proceedings.*
36. Maryland State Archives (Biographical Series), "Oswald Tilghman (1841–1932)," https://msa.maryland.gov/megafile/msa/speccol/sc3500/sc3520/012800/012815/html/12815collect.html.
37. *Harper's Weekly*, October 22 and 29, 1881; *Daily Graphic*, October 19 and 22, 1881.
38. *Brooklyn (NY) Union*, October 25, 1881.
39. Senate Report No. 1003.
40. United States War Department [hereafter USWD], *Annual Report*, vol. 1, 706.
41. Ibid., 708.
42. *Abington (VA) Weekly Virginian*, March 13, 1884.
43. *Goldsboro (NC) Messenger*, July 3, 1884.
44. USWD, *Annual Report*, vol. 1.
45. *Richmond (VA) Dispatch*, August 12, 1884.
46. *Norfolk (VA) Landmark*, August 17, 1884.
47. Wilson, "Yorktown Victory Monument."

Part II

48. *Norfolk (VA) Landmark*, January 25, 1885.
49. *Richmond (VA) Dispatch*, November 30, 1886.
50. *Weekly Virginian and Carolinian* (Norfolk, VA), February 3, 1887.
51. *Norfolk (VA) Landmark*, June 24, 1890.
52. *Report of the Secretary of War.*
53. *Richmond (VA) Dispatch*, April 13, 1902.
54. *Richmond (VA) Dispatch*, May 10, 1902.
55. *Richmond (VA) Dispatch*, July 20, 1902.
56. *Richmond (VA Times-Dispatch*, February 22, 1907.
57. *Statutes at Large*, vol. 33, part 1, session 3, Fifty-Eighth Congress, 1046.
58. Mark St. John, "'Meet Us on the War Path!': 1907 Jamestown Exposition Drew Millions to Hampton Roads," *Erickson Daily Press* (Newport News, VA), April 26, 2018.
59. *Official Blue Book.*
60. *Daily Press* (Newport News, VA), June 22, 1906.
61. *Alexandria (VA) Gazette*, October 12, 1906.
62. Dale, "Commercial Granites."
63. *Norfolk (VA) Landmark*, June 28, 1901.
64. *Daily Press* (Newport News, VA), April 30, 1913.
65. *Daily Press* (Newport News, VA), July 4, 1913.
66. *Daily Press* (Newport News, VA), August 19, 1909.
67. Thornton, *Penniman.*
68. *Daily Press* (Newport News, VA), August 4, 1917.
69. *Daily Press* (Newport News, VA), August 22, 1918.
70. *Daily Press* (Newport News, VA), January 4, 1920.
71. *Richmond (VA) Times-Dispatch*, November 17, 1921.
72. *Virginia Gazette* (Williamsburg), August 19, 1909.
73. *Richmond (VA) Times-Dispatch*, June 26, 1925.
74. *Richmond (VA) Times-Dispatch*, Friday, May 9, 1924.
75. *Richmond (VA) Times-Dispatch*, February 17, 1929.
76. *Richmond (VA) Times-Dispatch*, January 1, 1931.
77. USWD, *Annual Report*, vol. 1.
78. *Daily Press* (Newport News, VA), September 1, 1937.
79. *Daily Press* (Newport News, VA), July 30, 1942.

Part III

80. NPS and Robinson, *Outline of Development Colonial National Monument.*
81. *Daily Press* (Newport News, VA), October 13, 1943.
82. *Richmond (VA) Times-Dispatch*, November 17, 1943.
83. *Daily Press* (Newport News, VA), September 1, 1945.
84. *Daily Press* (Newport News, VA), February 9, 1947.
85. *Richmond (VA) Times-Dispatch*, February 13, 1947.
86. *Daily Press* (Newport News, VA), May 7, 1952.
87. *Daily Press* (Newport News, VA), February 3, 1949.
88. *Daily Press* (Newport News, VA), July 13, 1949.
89. *Richmond (VA) Times-Dispatch*, December 16, 1949.
90. *Daily Press* (Newport News, VA), October 20, 1951.
91. *Daily Press* (Newport News, VA), March 30, 1952.
92. *Richmond (VA) Times-Dispatch*, October 19, 1952.
93. *Daily Press* (Newport News, VA), April 16, 1953.
94. *Daily Press* (Newport News, VA), May 28, 1953.
95. *Richmond (VA) Times-Dispatch*, November 29, 1953.
96. *Daily Press* (Newport News, VA), November 30, 1953.
97. *Richmond (VA) Times-Dispatch*, December 11, 1953.
98. *Richmond (VA) Times-Dispatch*, December 17, 1953.
99. *Daily Press* (Newport News, VA), December 29, 1953
100. *Daily Press* (Newport News, VA), February 11, 1954
101. *Richmond (VA) Times-Dispatch*, April 4, 1954.
102. *Daily Press* (Newport News, VA), April 22, 1954.
103. *Richmond (VA) Times-Dispatch*, April 30, 1954.
104. *Richmond (VA) Times-Dispatch*, May 13, 1954.
105. *Daily Press* (Newport News, VA), December 9, 1954.
106. *Daily Press* (Newport News, VA), January 26, 1955.
107. U.S. Congress, *Hearings Before a Subcommittee of the Committee on Appropriations.*
108. *Richmond (VA) Times-Dispatch*, May 3, 1955.
109. *Richmond (VA) Times-Dispatch*, January 17, 1956.
110. *Richmond (VA) Times-Dispatch*, March 2, 1956.
111. *Richmond (VA) Times-Dispatch*, June 19, 1956.
112. *Daily Press* (Newport News, VA), August 5, 1956.
113. U.S. Congress, *Hearings Before a Subcommittee.*
114. *Daily Press* (Newport News, VA), December 29, 1968.
115. *Daily Press* (Newport News, VA), September 3, 1971.
116. *Richmond (VA) Times-Dispatch*, December 11, 1953.

Part IV

117. *Daily Press* (Newport News, VA), April 5, 1969.
118. *Daily Press* (Newport News, VA), August 11, 1961.
119. *Daily Press* (Newport News, VA), October 8, 1968.
120. *Daily Press* (Newport News, VA), March 20, 1977.
121. *Daily Press* (Newport News, VA), February 1, 1980.
122. *Miami (FL) Herald*, October 20, 1981.
123. Senate Document No. 8, 1986, Report of the Virginia Independence Bicentennial Commission 1966–1982
124. *Daily Press* (Newport News, VA), September 10, 1990.
125. *Telegraph-Forum* (Bucyrus, Ohio), June 29, 1993; *Washington Post*, June 28, 1993.
126. *Daily Press* (Newport News, VA), October 13, 1981.
127. *Daily Press* (Newport News, VA), May 28, 1990.
128. *Daily Press* (Newport News, VA), July 6, 1990.
129. *Daily Press* (Newport News, VA), August 16, 1991.
130. *Daily Press* (Newport News, VA), December 14, 1994.
131. Frank Wedekind (1864–1918), German playwright and dramatist.
132. *Daily Press* (Newport News, VA), August 16, 2018.
133. Van Brunt, "Historic Styles and Modern Architecture."
134. From the Cornerstone Ceremony, grand master of the Grand Lodge of Virginia, 1881.

Bibliography

Adams, Adeline. *John Quincy Adams Ward: An Appreciation*. New York: Gilliss Press, 1912.

Brandon, Edgar Ewing. *Lafayette, Guest of the Nation: A Contemporary Account of the Triumphal Tour of General Lafayette through the United States in 1824–1825, as Reported by the Local Newspapers*. Oxford, OH: Oxford Historical Press, 1951.

Chambers, Thomas A. *Memories of War: Visiting Battlegrounds and Bonefields in the Early American Republic*. 1st ed. Ithaca, NY: Cornell University Press, 2012.

The Chronicle, of the Early American Industries Association, Inc. 59, no. 2 (June 2006); no. 3 (September 2006); no. 4 (December 2006); 60, no.1 (2007).

Dale, T. Nelson. "The Commercial Granites of New England." *United States Geological Survey Bulletin* 738, 1923.

Du Hamel, William James Chamberlin. *An Address Read before the Maryland Historical Society on the Centennial of the Siege of Yorktown, VA*. New York: American Bank Note Co., 1880.

Eckenrode, H.J., Bryan Conrad and Virginia. *Official Guidebook of the Yorktown Sesquicentennial Celebration, October 16–19, 1931*. Richmond, VA: Yorktown Sesquicentennial Commission, 1931.

Folsom, Captain A.A. "Yorktown in 1854." William and Mary Quarterly 10, no. 4 (April 1902).

Foster, John. *A Sketch of the Tour of General Lafayette, On His Late Visit to the United States, 1824*. Portland, ME: Printed at the Statesman Office, by A.W. Thayer, 1824.

Gales and Seaton's Register of Debates in Congress. Vol. 10, Part 3, 4040, May 13, 1834. Washington, D.C.: 1835.

Greene, Jerome A. *The Guns of Independence: The Siege of Yorktown, 1781*. New York: Savas Beatie, 2005.

Harrison, S.A., and Oswald Tilghman. *Memoir of Lieut. Col. Tench Tilghman, Secretary and Aid to Washington: Together with an Appendix, Containing Revolutionary Journals and Letters, Hitherto Unpublished*. Albany, NY: J. Munsell, 1876.

Hiden, P.W. "Losses of York County Citizens in British Invasion, 1781." *William and Mary Quarterly* 7, no. 2 (April 1927).

A History of the Monument Erected by the U.S. Government to Commemorate the Close of the Revolutionary War, At Yorktown, October 19th, 1781. Philadelphia: Dewey & Eakins, Printers, 1890.

Jameson, David. "To Level the Works at York…A Letter of David Jameson" (July 16, 1783). Edited by Donald O. Dewey. *Virginia Magazine of History and Biography* 71 (1963): 150–51.

Jamestown Exposition Company. *Jamestown Exposition, April 26th to Nov. 30th, 1907*. Norfolk, VA: W.T. Barron & Co., 1907.

Jamestown-Williamsburg-Yorktown Celebration Commission. *The Three Hundred Fiftieth Anniversary of Jamestown, 1607–1957: Final Report to the President and Congress*. Washington, D.C.: Government Printing Office, 1958.

Johnston, Henry P., ed. *The Correspondence and Public Papers of John Jay, 1782–1793*. Vol. 3. New York: G.P. Putnam's Sons, 1891.

Laird & Lee's Guide to Historic Virginia and the Jamestown Centennial: Full Statistics and Itinerary. Chicago: Laird & Lee, 1907.

La Rochefoucauld-Liancourt, F., and H. Neuman. *Travels through the United States of North America: The Country of the Iroquois, and Upper Canada, in the Years 1795, 1796, and 1797*. 2nd ed. London: R. Phillips, 1800.

Latrobe, Benjamin Henry, Engineer. *An Essay on Landscape, Explained in Tinted Drawings*. Vol. 1, *1798–1799*. Richmond, VA, 1799.

Levasseur, Auguste. *Lafayette in America in 1824 and 1825: Or, Journal of Travels in the United States*. New York: White, Gallaher & White, 1829.

Lossing, Benson John. *The Pictorial Field-book of the Revolution: Or, Illustrations, by Pen and Pencil, of the History, Biography, Scenery, Relics, and Traditions of the War for Independence*. New York: Harper & Brothers, 1850.

McSpadden, J. Walker. *Famous Sculptors of America*. New York: Dodd, Mead and Company, 1924.

National Archives. Papers of the Continental Congress, No. 78, XIII. 285–288. https://catalog.archives.gov/id/1938489.

National Park Service and William M. Robinson Jr. *Outline of Development for Colonial National Monument.* Washington, D.C.: United States Department of the Interior, 1933.

The Official Blue Book of the Jamestown Ter-Centennial Exposition, the Only Authorized History of the Celebration. Norfolk, VA: Colonial Publishing Company, 1907.

Patton, Jacob Harris. *Yorktown: a Compendious Account of the Campaign of the Allied French and American Forces, Resulting in the Surrender of Cornwallis and the Close of the American Revolution; the Succeeding Events, to the Treaty of Peace; and the Celebration of the Centennial Anniversary of the Surrender at Yorktown.* New York: Fords, Howard & Hulbert, 1882.

The Peninsula Campaign of 1862: Yorktown to the Seven Days. Campbell, CA: Savas Woodbury, 1993.

Petition of Certain Citizens of York County, for a Railroad From Richmond to Yorktown. Richmond: State of Virginia, 1852.

Pierce, Mildred Beatty. *Shreds and Patches of History: Found Mostly in Virginia.* East Aurora, NY: Roycrofters, 1906.

Proceedings of the Meeting At Yorktown, Preparatory to a National Centennial Celebration of the Surrender of Lord Cornwallis: With Correspondence Had in Pursuance Thereof. Richmond, VA: R.E. Frayser, 1879.

Rawle, Anna, and William Broek Rawle. "A Loyalist's Account of Certain Occurrences in Philadelphia after Cornwallis's Surrender at Yorktown." *Pennsylvania Magazine of History and Biography* 16, no. 1 (April 1892).

Report of the Secretary of War; Being Part of The Message and Documents Communicated to the Two Houses of Congress at the Beginning of the Second Session of the Fifty-Second Congress, Vol. 1. Washington, D.C.: Government Printing Office, 1892.

Scott, Robert Gourmain. *To the Public.* Richmond, VA: R.G. Scott, 1827.

Senate Report No. 1003. *Report of the Commission Created in Accordance with a Joint Resolution of Congress, Approved March 3, 1881, Providing for the Erection of a Monument at Yorktown, VA., Commemorative of the Surrender of Lord Cornwallis.* Washington, D.C.: Government Printing Office, 1883.

Smith, Margaret P. Crooks. *Old Yorktown and Its History.* Richmond, VA: Richmond Press, 1920.

The Statutes at Large of the United States of America from April 1879 to March 1881. Vol. 21. Washington, D.C.: Government Printing Office, n.d.

The Statutes at Large of the United States of America from November 1903 to March 1905. Vol. 33. Washington, D.C.: Government Printing Office, n.d.

Stevens, John Austin. *Yorktown Centennial Handbook: Historical and Topographical Guide to the Yorktown Peninsula, Richmond, James River, and Norfolk.* New York: Printed for the author by C.A. Coffin & Rogers, 1881.

Stone, E. Martin. *Our French Allies: Rochambeau and His Army, Lafayette and His Devotion, D'Estaing, De Ternay, Barras, De Grasse, and Their Fleets, in the Great War of the American Revolution from 1778–1782, including Military Operations in Rhode Island, the Surrender of Yorktown, Sketches of French and American Officers, and Incidents of Social Life in Newport, Providence, and Elsewhere; with Numerous Illustrations.* Providence, RI: Providence Press Company, 1884.

Thornton, Rosemary. *Penniman.* 2nd ed. N.p.: Sheryl M. Howie, 2020.

Trudell, Clyde Francis. *Colonial Yorktown: An Exploration through One of America's Most Richly Historic Towns: Its Houses, Heroes, and Legends.* Gettysburg, PA: Thomas Publications: 1971.

———. *Colonial Yorktown: Being a Brief Historie of the Place; Together with Something of Its Houses and Publick Buildings*. Richmond, VA: Dietz Press, 1938.

U.S. Congress. *House Committee on Military Affairs. Yorktown Battle Ground Park: Hearing Before the Committee On Military Affairs, House of Representatives, Sixty-eighth Congress, First [–Second] Session, On H.R. 8521, to Establish a National Military Park at the Battle Field of Yorktown*. Washington, D.C.: Government Printing Office, 1924–25.

———. *House Committee on the Public Lands. Creating the Colonial National Monument: Hearings Before the Committee On the Public Lands, House of Representatives, Seventy-First Congress, Second Session On H.R. 8424, to Provide for the Creation of the Colonial National Monument In Virginia*. Washington: Government Printing Office, 1930.

———. *Interior Department and Related Agencies Appropriations for 1956., Hearings before a Subcommittee on Appropriations, Eighty-Fourth Congress, First Session on H.R. 5085, Making Appropriations for the Department of the Interior and Related Agencies for the Fiscal Year Ending June 30, 1956, and for Other Purposes*. Washington, D.C.: Government Printing Office, 1955.

United States. Naval Facilities Engineering Command. Atlantic Division, et al. *Cast Down Your Bucket Where You Are: an Ethnohistorical Study of the African-American Community On the Lands of the Yorktown Naval Weapons Station, 1865–1918*. Williamsburg, VA: The Center, 1992.

United States War Department. *Annual Reports of the Secretary of War*. Vols. 1–4. Washington, D.C.: Government Printing Office, 1881–1895.

Van Brunt, Henry. *Greek Lines and Other Architectural Essays*. Boston: Houghton Mifflin, 1893.

———. "Historic Styles and Modern Architecture." In *Architecture and Society* edited by Henry Van Brunt and William A. Cole. Cambridge, MA: Harvard University Press, 1969.

Ward, R.D. *An Account of General La Fayette's Visit to Virginia, in the Years 1824–25: Containing Full Circumstantial Reports of His Receptions in Washington, Alexandria, Mount Vernon, Yorktown, Williamsburg, Norfolk, Richmond.* Richmond, VA: West, Johnston & Co., 1881.

Weld, Isaac. *Travels through the States of North America, and the Provinces of Upper and Lower Canada, During the Years 1795, 1796, and 1797.* 3rd ed. London: Printed for J. Stockdale, Piccadilly, 1800.

Wilson, Richard Guy. "Yorktown Victory Monument." Society of Architectural Historians, https://sah-archipedia.org/buildings/VA-01-HR45.9.

Yorktown Centennial Commission. *Official Programme of the Yorktown Centennial Celebration: October 18, 19, 20, 21, 1881. Under the Joint Resolution of Congress of June 7, 1880.* Washington, D.C.: F.T. Wilson, 1881.

———. *Report of the Commission Created in Accordance with a Joint Resolution of Congress, Approved March 3, 1881: Providing for the Erection of a Monument at Yorktown, Va., Commemorative of the Surrender of Lord Cornwallis.* Washington, D.C.: Government Printing Office, 1883.

———. *See! See! See! Guide to Jamestown Exposition, Historic Virginia, and Washington.* Washington, D.C.: B.S. Adams, 1907.

Yorktown Sesquicentennial Association. *Official Program of the Yorktown Sesquicentennial, Yorktown, Virginia, 1931.* Richmond, VA: Yorktown Sesquicentennial Association, 1931.

Yorktown Sesquicentennial Commission, and Schuyler Otis Bland. *The Yorktown Sesquicentennial: Proceedings of the United States Yorktown Sesquicentennial Commission in Connection with the Celebration of the Siege of Yorktown, 1781.* Washington, D.C.: U.S. Government Printing Office, 1932.

Index

A

Abbott, Superintendent 109, 110
allegory 49, 130, 133
aluminum headdress 119, 122
Anderson, Robert 23, 30, 35
APVA 70, 72, 74, 127
Arthur, President Chester A. 40, 41

B

bicentennial 135–160
Bland, Otis 82, 97, 99, 100, 101
Blow, George P. 74, 79, 80, 137

C

carbide chisel 105
caryatids 47, 51, 60
CCC 89, 90, 95, 97
cement 48
cemetery 25, 67, 114
centennial 13–62
Chesapeake 9, 13, 14, 19, 28, 52, 74, 86, 141
Civil War 25, 55, 66, 67, 82, 95, 114, 130, 138, 152
Colonial Dames of Virginia 74
Colonial Williamsburg 135, 137, 150
commission of artists 28, 30, 36, 44, 46, 48, 62, 130
Confederates 25, 35, 38, 153
contraband 25
contracts 47, 54, 85
cornerstone 37
Craighill, William Price 28, 33, 37, 40, 42, 45, 53, 60, 65, 162
criticism 62, 66, 69, 147

D

DAR 99, 100, 106, 109, 118
DeNeufville, John S. 49, 60, 112, 122
derrick 37, 47, 51

de Weldon, Felix 140, 141, 142, 143
drum 47

E

editorial comments 114

F

Ferris, Judge 79, 81, 83
foundation 37
Franklin, Benjamin 15, 16, 89, 122

G

Gloucester 9, 19, 25, 106
Goode, John 27
gunmetal 48

H

Hallowell Granite Company 45, 46, 47, 48
Hansen, Oskar 101, 102, 104, 105, 106, 107, 108, 109, 110, 111, 112, 113, 114, 115, 116, 117, 118, 119, 124, 126, 128, 129, 130
Hunt, Richard M. 28, 30, 45, 52, 55, 60, 62, 104

I

injury 49

J

James River 25
Jamestown Exposition 70
Jensen, Ben F. 111, 112, 113, 117

K

keeper 53, 64, 65, 69

L

Lafayette, Marquis de 9, 14, 20, 22, 24, 35, 55, 63, 140, 161
Latrobe, Benjamin 18
Libertas Americana (medal) 16
lightning rod 119, 122
Lossing, Benson J. 23

M

Manor Hotel 80, 83, 90, 137
Masonic 37, 39
Mathews, Mary 142
McKay, Douglas 108, 111, 117, 119
McKean, Thomas 13
model 30

N

Nelson, Secretary 10, 18, 35, 83, 137
Nelson, Thomas 19, 20, 23, 74
Nelson, William 22
Norfolk 27
North Carolina Granite 104

O

obelisk 16, 21, 67, 68, 69, 149

P

Philadelphia 13, 27, 84, 161, 169

plaster 51, 74, 99, 102, 141, 142
Pocahontas 73, 85, 111
proposals 16, 36, 44, 45

Q

quarry 47

R

recognition block 128
Rochambeau, General 11, 14, 21, 140
Roosevelt, Franklin 70, 72, 89, 95

S

safety 63, 107, 110, 111, 146
Scott, Robert G. 20, 21
secretary of the interior 99, 105, 108, 110, 111, 150
sesquicentennial 63–94
Shaw, John W. 67, 68
Statue of Liberty 27, 28, 30
Stinchfield Quarry 47, 124
Surrender Field 84, 112, 113, 141, 142
sword 14, 19, 21, 25, 101

T

Taft, William Howard 70, 72
Temple Farm 35
tercentennial 70, 160
Tilghman, Tench 13, 41, 79, 84, 135, 157, 161, 162
tourism 137
Truman, President Harry S 102

U

USS *Yorktown* 91

V

Van Brunt, Henry 28, 29, 55, 104
Victorian style 105, 130

W

War Department 28, 78, 81, 104
Ward, J.Q.A. 28, 51, 60, 122, 130, 147
Washington, D.C. 29, 102, 107, 124, 142
Washington, George 9, 13, 16, 39
Whitney, Charles S. 114, 115
Wilson, President Woodrow 77
wind pressure 46, 89, 115

Y

York River 20, 51, 75, 77, 84, 91, 99, 106, 140, 150
Yorktown Centennial Association 27, 35, 38, 44
Yorktown Historical Society 83
Yorktown World Forum 80

About the Author

Maria Hepner is a raconteur whose ties to the history of York County, Virginia, reach back fourteen generations. The lifetimes of family oral history, and the benefit of being a native of an area that is the genesis of Colonial and Revolutionary War history aided her research into long-overlooked legends and stories. Miss Hepner spent over fourteen years associated with Colonial National Historical Park, employed in the Visitor Center Museum Shop and serving as a seasonal park guide, and volunteer.